# Quick
# GIFTS and DECOR

*Nancy Zieman and Gail Brown*

Oxmoor
House®

# Quick Gifts and Decor

by Nancy Zieman and Gail Brown
from the "Sewing with Nancy" series
©1998 by Nancy Zieman, Gail Brown, and Oxmoor House, Inc.
Book Division of Southern Progress Corporation
P.O. Box 2463, Birmingham, Alabama 35201

Published by Oxmoor House, Inc., and Leisure Arts, Inc.

Library of Congress Catalog Number: 98-65709
Hardcover ISBN: 0-8487-1678-7
Softcover ISBN: 0-8487-1679-5
Manufactured in the United States of America
Third Printing 2004

Editor-in-Chief: Nancy Fitzpatrick Wyatt
Senior Crafts Editor: Susan Ramey Cleveland
Senior Editor, Editorial Services: Olivia Kindig Wells
Art Director: James Boone

## Quick Gifts and Decor
Editor: Lois Martin
Copy Editor: Anne S. Dickson
Editorial Assistants: Cecile Y. Nierodzinski and
    Kaye Howard Smith
Associate Art Director: Cynthia R. Cooper
Designer: Larry Hunter
Director, Production and Distribution: Phillip Lee
Associate Production Manager: Theresa L. Beste
Senior Photographer: John O'Hagan
Photographer: Keith Glasgow
Photo Stylist: Linda Baltzell Wright
Illustrator: Rochelle Stibb
Editorial Assistance, Nancy's Notions: Betty Hanneman

To order additional publications, call
1-800-765-6400.
For more books to enrich your life, visit
**oxmoorhouse.com**

The editor thanks Mark McDowell and the staff of the Sewing Machine Mart in Homewood, Alabama, for lending the Pfaff sewing machine and serger used in photography.

# Nancy and Gail's Top 10 Time-Finders

Each project in this book can be finished quickly—just check out the charts at the beginning of each chapter to see which ones are the quickest to sew. We've also given you Bonus Projects—items you can make by changing slightly the instructions for another project. However, just finding time to sew can be a challenge. Some of our favorite time-finders may help you discover minutes hidden in your busy days.

1. Divide and conquer! Sew in 10- to 20-minute sessions, rather than waiting for the elusive two-hour, uninterrupted time block. (Nancy devoted an entire book to this concept, called *10•20•30 Minutes to Sew*, also published by Oxmoor House.)

2. Cut out, sew, quilt, and craft where the action is in your home. The most productive sewers we know work where they also cook, serve meals, or watch television.

3. Sort through sewing drawers, closets, and boxes, and give away fabric and notions that you probably won't use. You'll be inspired by your streamlined inventory and more efficient when sewing your next project.

4. Leave your sewing machine and serger out, ready for stitching.

5. Set up your sewing machine (and serger) with invisible or neutral-colored thread. Doing so minimizes time-consuming thread changes—plus you'll be ready for last-minute alteration emergencies.

6. Don't be discouraged by unfinished projects. Creative people *always* have them. If you become stalled, move to a more easily completed project. You'll jump-start your sewing enthusiasm and momentum.

7. Leave unfinished projects where they're visible. If you stash them away in bags and closets, you might forget them. Gail hangs garments in need of finishing or altering in full view as a daily reminder; she puts partially finished projects in see-through plastic bins stacked on a work table. Try putting almost-finished decorator items in place—an appliqué pinned to your couch pillow reminds you to finish that project!

8. Stitch, craft, or quilt while you talk on the telephone. Long telephone handset cords or cordless phones make this easier. Our friends and relatives have grown accustomed to hearing the whir of a serger or sewing machine in the background. To concentrate on sewing without interruptions, turn on an answering machine.

9. With the help of family and friends, stage your own sewing retreat. Gail's husband, John, is her hero when he announces, "I'm taking the kids and dog to the beach for a couple of days." Home alone with her sewing machine and serger, she can actually finish several projects.

10. Relish the sanity and lowered stress of any moments, however few, spent sewing.

*Nancy Zieman*      *Gail Brown*

# Contents

*Finish your **Festive Packages** with this Jelly Roll accent, page 120.*

*Make this adorable Tot's Getup from towels. You'll find it in **Timesaving Transformations**, page 22.*

*Make this Wish Pillow for that special child. It's featured in **Pillows from the Heart**, page 57.*

*Elegant Gift Sacks like these are shown in **Festive Packages**, page 118.*

*Stitch a holiday Mantel Scarf from **Celebrations**, page 92.*

# Timesaving
## Transformations

# From Place Mats

**Diagram C**

You're in a hurry to gather your travel gear. Where do you put your hot curling iron? Even before the iron has cooled, pack it safely away from heat-sensitive fabrics and containers in this clever caddy, made quickly from a place mat.

## Curling Iron Caddy

### Gather Supplies
- 1 rectangular place mat
- ⅓ yard (0.3 m) heat-resistant fabric
- Thread to match

### Create Curling Iron Caddy
1. Mark placement lines for the pockets.
- Fold the place mat in half, right sides together, aligning short ends *(Diagram A)*.
- Fold the place mat again, so that the short edges extend slightly beyond the first fold.

You have now folded the place mat approximately in fourths *(Diagram B)*.

**Diagram A**          **Diagram B**

- Pin along the second set of fold lines. Unfold the place mat *(Diagram C)*.

2. Stitch heat-resistant fabric to the place mat.
- Measure the area between the pins, and cut a rectangle of heat-resistant fabric to this measurement.

### Note from Nancy

We used Iron Quick Teflon-coated fabric as the lining for the curling iron caddy. You can use this versatile, heat-resistant fabric in other quick projects, too, such as casserole carriers, oven mitts, and hot pads.

- Stitch ¼" (6 mm) from all raw edges of the heat-resistant fabric. Press under the ¼" (6 mm) seam allowance.
- Center the heat-resistant fabric on the right side of the place mat, between the pin markings. (This fabric is slightly smaller than the marked area.)
- Topstitch the heat-resistant fabric to the place mat along all four sides *(Diagram D)*.

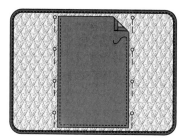

**Diagram D**

3. Stitch the curling iron pocket.
- Fold the place mat in half, right sides together, aligning the short ends. Pin at the second set of fold lines.
- Draw a line between the pin markings, and stitch along the line to the lower edge. Pivot, and stitch across the bottom to create a pocket *(Diagram E)*.

**Diagram E**

4. Create the side pockets.
- Refold the short ends of the place mat to meet beyond the first fold. The bias-trim edges should meet.
- At the top of the caddy, fold each corner at a 45° angle. Unfold the caddy and stitch the corners to the side pocket, along the bias trim *(Diagram F)*.

**Diagram F**

- Refold the caddy, pin in place, and stitch the bias trim together along the caddy side and lower edges *(Diagram G)*.

**Diagram G**

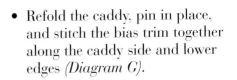

*Tip from Gail*

If the layers of the caddy are thick, turn the sewing machine handwheel manually to prevent breaking the needle.

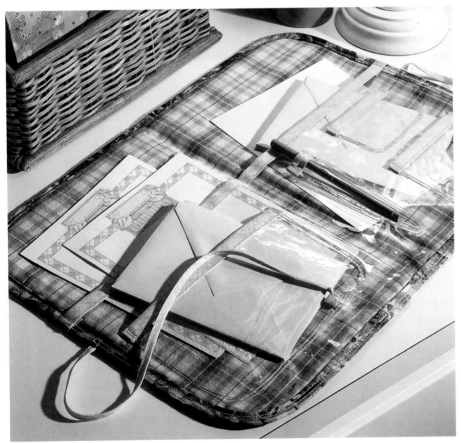

*Filled with writing papers, pens, envelopes, stamps, and a pocket calendar, this portable organizer makes a great gift or on-the-go office.*

# Stationery Organizer

## Gather Supplies
- ¼ yard (0.25 m) clear vinyl
- 1 place mat
- 1 yard (0.95 m) of ½"-wide (1.3 cm-wide) ribbon for ties
- Optional: ½ yard (0.5 m) bias tape
- Optional: Tear-away nonwoven stabilizer or tissue paper

## Create Stationery Organizer
1. Cut an 8" x 18" (20.5 cm x 46 cm) rectangle of vinyl.
2. Stitch coordinating or matching bias tape across one lengthwise edge of vinyl. Or turn under a ¼" (6 mm) hem and edgestitch.
3. Create small vinyl pockets.
- Cut vinyl pockets ½" (1.3 cm) wider and longer than needed.
- Place the pockets on the larger vinyl section on either side of the center.

*(Continued on page 10)*

- Edgestitch ¼" (6 mm) from the sides and the bottoms of the pockets.

4. Place the large vinyl pocket section on the place mat, lining up the unhemmed lengthwise edge along one lengthwise edge of the place mat. To avoid creating pinholes in the vinyl, use tape or paper clips to hold the edges in place.

5. Stitch around the edge of the vinyl on the three unfinished sides, stitching close to the place mat's binding.

6. Stitch down the center of the vinyl to create pockets for storing stationery *(Diagram A)*.

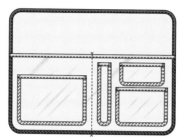

**Diagram A**

7. Cut the ribbon into two equal lengths. Turn under one short edge of each ribbon, and topstitch to the right side of the organizer, centering each ribbon on the short sides of the place mat *(Diagram B)*.

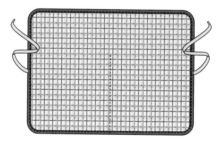

**Diagram B**

# Sewing Organizer

## Gather Supplies

- 1 place mat
- Fabric marking pen
- 4 (1-gallon) resealable storage bags
- 4–6 (1-quart) resealable storage bags
- 4–6 (1-pint) resealable storage bags
- Thread to match
- ½ yard (0.50 m) of 1"-wide (2.5 cm-wide) decorative ribbon
- 1 yard (0.95 m) of ½"-wide (1.3 cm-wide) ribbon for ties

## Create Sewing Organizer

1. Fold the place mat in half, wrong sides together, aligning the short ends. Using a fabric marking pen, draw a line along the inside fold line.

2. Stack the storage bags on the place mat.

- Stack a gallon storage bag with the resealable edge 1" (2.5 cm) from the short edge of the place mat. Use tape or paper clips to secure. Repeat on the opposite end of the place mat.
- Stack the second set of gallon storage bags, with the resealable edges 3" (7.5 cm) from the ends.
- Stack and stagger the quart- and pint-size storage bags, with the resealable edges 5" to 6" (12.5 cm to 15 cm) from the ends *(Diagram AA)*.

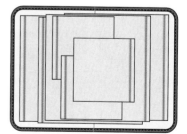

**Diagram AA**

*Create ideal storage space for your favorite notions and sewing tools by using the size and number of storage bags you like.*

3. Mark the center line across the storage bags. Stitch through all layers, joining the storage bags to the place mat.

### *Note from Nancy*

To customize this organizer, change the size and number of storage bags. For example, if you want to store silk ribbon, use pint-size bags rather than gallon-size bags.

4. Trim the bottoms of the storage bags on either side of the stitching line *(Diagram BB)*.

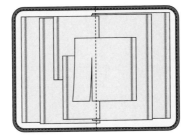

**Diagram BB**

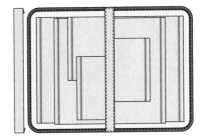

**Diagram CC**

5. To secure the storage bags, stitch the ribbon to the place mat.
- Turn under the ends of 1"-wide (2.5 cm-wide) ribbon, making the length fit the width of the place mat. Trim excess ribbon.
- Center the ribbon over the stitching line.
- Edgestitch on all sides of the ribbon *(Diagram CC)*.

6. To add a ribbon tie closure, follow Step 7 of Stationery Organizer (page 10).

# From Napkins

*Rollup "lapkins" make setting up for a buffet simple, yet elegant. Sturdy enough to hold tableware, they spread open when emptied to protect laps. Sew a set as a housewarming or holiday gift, or as a lovely accent for your own get-togethers.*

# Buffet Lapkins

## Gather Supplies

- 2 napkins, at least 15" (38 cm) square, for each lapkin. Use identical or contrasting napkins, but each pair must be same size.
- 1¾ yard (1.60 m) of ½"- to ¾"-wide (1.3 cm- to 2 cm-wide) stitchable, paper-backed fusible web strips, or 1 small bottle liquid fusible web
- 1 yard (0.95 m) of ½"- to ¾"-wide (1.3 cm- to 2 cm-wide) grosgrain ribbon, in matching or contrasting color
- Thread to match
- 1 small bottle seam sealant

## Create Buffet Lapkins

1. Fuse the napkins *(Diagram A)*.

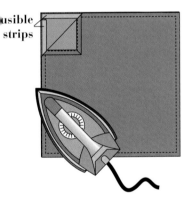

**Diagram A**

- Working from the wrong side, position fusible web strips on the edges of one napkin. Fuse in place, following manufacturer's directions.
- Remove the paper backing.
- With wrong sides together and edges even, fuse the napkins.
- If you prefer, use a liquid fusible instead of web (see *Note from Nancy,* page 14).

2. Prepare the double-layer napkin and ribbon ties for stitching.
- Fold the napkin in half to form a triangle.
- Fold one of the top points inside to meet the center fold *(Diagram B)*.

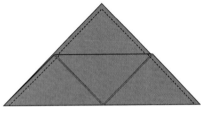

**Diagram B**

- Fold the ribbon in half. Tuck about 1" (2.5 cm) of the folded end of the ribbon into the right lower edge opening. Pin in place.
- Pin the napkin layers together.
3. Topstitch to secure the layers.
- Use the napkin hemline as a guide to stitch the two unfolded edges.
- Catch the ribbon in the top-stitching.

4. Topstitch to create knife, fork, and spoon pockets *(Diagram C)*.

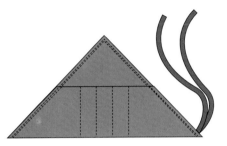

**Diagram C**

5. Trim the ribbon ends diagonally, and dab with seam sealant to prevent raveling.

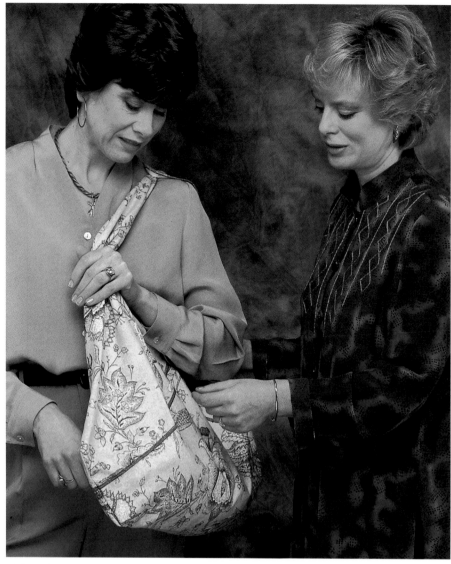

## Create Soft Tote

1. To line the center section of the tote, fuse the wrong sides of two napkins to each other *(Diagram A)*.

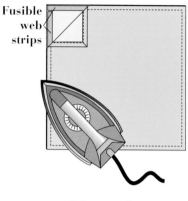

**Fusible web strips**

**Diagram A**

- Working from the wrong side, position fusible web strips on the sides of one napkin. Following the manufacturer's instructions, fuse the strips in place.
- Remove the paper backing.
- With wrong sides together, fuse the napkins.
- If you prefer, use a liquid fusible instead of the web.

### Note from Nancy

Liquid fusibles, like Liqui Fuse™ Liquid Fusible Web™, are new to the sewing market and really save time. Simply apply a fine line of the liquid to the wrong side of the napkin edge and let dry. (I often speed drying with a hand-held hair dryer.) Then, with wrong sides facing and edges aligned, press to fuse the napkins together.

2. Determine the seaming style *(Diagram B)*. If the napkins have serged seams, you can zigzag the butted seam (**a**), or you can overlap the edges and straightstitch (**b**). If the napkins have traditional

*Take advantage of this carryall for toting workout clothes, overnight gear, or baby items. Gail (left) and Nancy like this tote because it's soft and folds nearly flat, so you can pack it in a suitcase or hang it up to use as a laundry bag or diaper holder.*

## Soft Tote

### Gather Supplies
- 4 napkins, at least 15" (38 cm) square. Prints and colors can match or contrast, but napkins must be the same size. Napkins that are 20" (51 cm) square yield a tote about 28" (71 cm) square. The larger the napkins used, the larger the tote.

- 1¾ yard (1.60 m) stitchable, paper-backed fusible web strips, ½" to ¾" (1.3 cm to 2 cm) wide, for 15" (38 cm) napkins. (You need more fusible web for larger napkins.) Or substitute 1 small bottle of liquid fusible web.
- Thread to match
- Scraps of stable, fusible, non-woven interfacing
- Optional: 3 (⅝"-wide or 1.5 cm-wide) buttons

seams, overlap the edges and straightstitch (**c**).

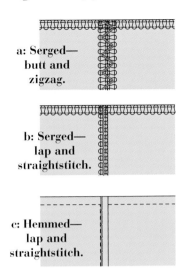

a: Serged— butt and zigzag.

b: Serged— lap and straightstitch.

c: Hemmed— lap and straightstitch.

**Diagram B**

3. Using the chosen seaming style, sew the tote together.

• Sew the three napkins together, meeting **a** to **a** and **b** to **b** as shown in *Diagram C*. When stitched, all three napkins should be right side up, with the lined napkin in the center.

• Sew side **c** to side **c**, stitching toward the corner *(Diagram D)*. Leave about 1" to 2" (2.5 cm to 5 cm) of the seam open, which you'll trim after mitering.

*By fusing two napkins, you create a sturdy bottom for this tote.*

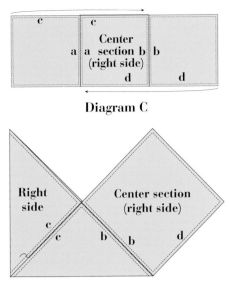

**Diagram C**

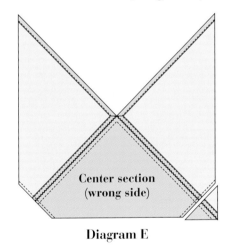

**Diagram D**

• Sew side **d** to side **d**, stitching toward the corner. Leave about 1" to 2" (2.5 cm to 5.1 cm) of the seam open.

4. Assemble the tote using your chosen seaming style.

• Miter the tote corners. Align the seams, right sides together. Straightstitch across the corners.

• Trim the excess and finish the seam allowances *(Diagram E)*.

**Center section (wrong side)**

**Diagram E**

5. Form the handle.

• Reinforce the corners with a 2" square of stable, fusible, non-woven interfacing *(Diagram F)*.

• Lap the top corners about 1¾" (4.5 cm) and edgestitch *(Diagram G)*.

• Or stitch a buttonhole in one corner, and sew a corresponding button on the other corner *(Diagram H)*.

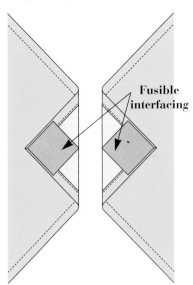

Fusible interfacing

**Diagram F**

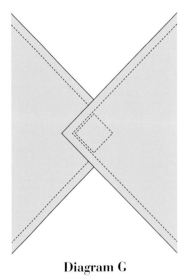

**Diagram G**

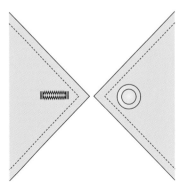

**Diagram H**

*This unusual starburst design suits just about any table size or shape—round, oval, rectangular, or square. You can also drape this versatile accessory over a piano.*

# Starburst Table Scarf

## Gather Supplies

- 6 napkins, at least 15" (38 cm) square, of the same design. Checks, stripes, borders, and fringed designs work well.

Napkins 15" (38 cm) square yield scarf about 45" (115 cm) in diameter, point to point.
- Thread to match
- Optional: Fabric marking pen
- Optional: Grid Works (pattern paper with special coating on nongridded side that bonds temporarily to fabric without leaving residue)

*Tip from Gail*

When choosing napkins, be sure they are all the same size. If you're using napkins with a border print, make sure that all the borders are the same distance from the napkin edge.

# Create Starburst Table Scarf

1. Transfer the pattern from page 142 to Grid Works or plain paper. Extend the lines to fit your napkin.
2. Pin or press the pattern to the right side of one napkin. Press the sides of the napkin to match the pattern angles. Cut out, allowing ½" (1.3 cm) seam allowances (*Diagram A*). Repeat for the remaining five napkins.

**Diagram A**

*Tip from Gail*

To match checks, stripes, and borders perfectly, use the first cut napkin as the pattern for the remaining sections. Place the cut section on an uncut napkin, aligning motifs. If border-print inconsistencies make matching difficult at the top center, cut the sections smaller, eliminating the center motif.

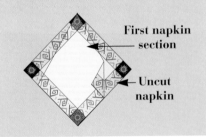

First napkin section

Uncut napkin

3. Assemble the scarf halves.
- Press under the seam allowances on two napkin sections.

*Tip from Gail*

Adjusting the lap depth at the seam lines is essential for your scarf to lie flat. By checking the fit of scarf sections before seaming, you can compensate for size and weave variations among the napkins. Rather than following the pattern shape exactly, you may need to alter it slightly to suit your napkins.

- Working in sets of three, align the seam lines and pin. If patterns don't match, or if the scarf does not lie flat, repin the seam lines, adjusting the lap depth as needed.
- Optional: Use a fabric marking pen to mark both sides of the seam lines.
- Using the press-markings or pen markings as a guide, seam two sets of three napkins to form two halves (*Diagram B*).

**Diagram B**

- Press the seams flat.
- Straightstitch, zigzag, or serge the seam allowances together, about ⅜" (1 cm) from the seam lines. Trim excess allowances close to the stitching.
4. Assemble the scarf.
- Press under the seam allowances along the unseamed edge of one half, and lap it over the other (*Diagram C*). Deepen the lap if necessary to flatten the scarf. Press and pin.

*Tip from Gail*

Because you cut these seams on the bias, they're prone to stretch no matter how carefully you handle them. This stretching causes seams to curve and keeps the scarf from lying flat. After seaming, lay one half of the scarf on your pressing board to check for flatness. Press out curves by deepening the lap, which widens the seam. Just be sure your motifs still match. Then, using the new press-markings as guides, restitch the seam(s).

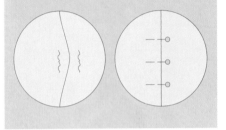

- Using the press-markings as guides, seam two halves together. If your scarf doesn't lie flat, repress and restitch as needed (see *Tip from Gail*, above).
5. Optional: Outline the star shape by decoratively machine-stitching ½" (1.3 cm) from the outer edge.

**Diagram C**

# From Potholders

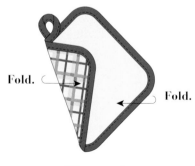

*Stitched in mere minutes, this case makes scissors easier to locate.*

## Eyeglass Holder

### Gather Supplies
- 1 potholder
- Thread to match

### Create Eyeglass Holder
1. Fold the potholder in half.
2. To create the pocket, stitch down the side edge and around the bottom curve to the center fold *(Diagram)*.

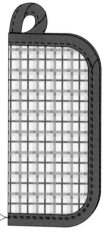

**Diagram**

*Anyone can easily transform a basic potholder into an eyeglass holder. This handy holder is practical, too, because the quilting provides protective padding for eyeglasses.*

## Scissors Case

### Gather Supplies
- 1 potholder
- Thread to match
- Optional: decorative ribbon, flowers, or other trim

### Create Scissors Case
1. Position the potholder's loop at the top to serve as a hanger. If the loop is centered on one side, choose a corner on the loop side to serve as the top of the case.
2. Fold the potholder into a cone shape *(Diagram A)*. Handstitch the edges together.
3. Optional: Place ribbon, flowers, or other decorative trim at the top, where the two sections overlap *(Diagram B)*. Handstitch or glue trim in place.

Fold. Fold.

**Diagram A**

**Diagram B**

# From Sheets

*Protect clothing while cooking, crafting, or doing household chores, with this flattering, adjust-to-fit-just-about-anyone cover-up.*

## Gather Supplies

- 1 twin flat sheet (66" x 96" or 167.5 cm x 244 cm). 1 sheet yields 1 adult and 1 child's cover-up (see Bonus Project on page 21). Overall patterns or stripes with contrasting borders work well. We used a sheet with a 7"-wide (18 cm-wide) reversible border.
- Tailor's chalk
- Thread to match
- Pencil and pattern paper or tracing paper
- 1 yard (0.95 m) of ½"-wide (1.3 cm-wide) grosgrain ribbon or any durable, washable ribbon
- Optional: ¾ yard (0.70 m) of ½"-wide (1.3 cm-wide) grosgrain ribbon for child's cover-up
- Optional: Bias Tape Maker

*(Continued on page 20)*

## Create Quick Cover-up

1. Cut the cover-up from the sheet.
- Use chalk to mark a rectangle 71" (180.5 cm) long and 40" to 46" (102 cm to 117 cm) wide *(Diagram A)*. This makes a cover-up 31" (78.5 cm) long and 36" to 42" (91.5 cm to 107 cm) wide. You can make necessary length adjustments in Step 2.

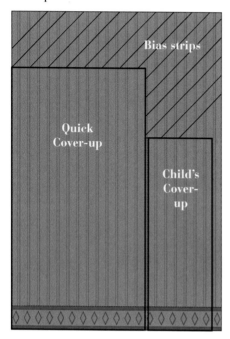

**Diagram A**

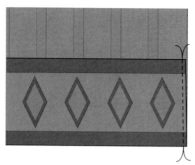

**Diagram B**

3. Make a 1½" (3.8 cm) double hem on the short cut end of the rectangle (the back). See page 135 for directions. Topstitch 1" (2.5 cm) from the hemline fold.
4. Cut the neckline opening.
- Fold the cover-up in half crosswise, with wrong sides together and hemlines even. Pin-mark the fold to indicate shoulder lines *(Diagram C)*.

**Diagram C**

- Unfold the cover-up and refold it lengthwise, wrong sides together. Pin-mark the fold to indicate center front and center back.
- Trace the neckline pattern from page 138 onto pattern paper or tracing paper.
- Line up the neckline pattern with the shoulder and the center front markings. Cut the neckline opening *(Diagram D)*.

**Diagram D**

5. Appliqué a design under the front neckline (see page 128 for directions). We used cutouts from sheet remnants, but you could use a motif cut from another fabric.
6. Make bias binding.
- Use a Bias Tape Maker. (See page 130 for binding tips.) Cut a bias strip of sheet fabric 2" (5 cm) wide by the neckline circumference plus 1" or 2.5 cm (about 31" or 78.5 cm). Pull the strip through the Bias Tape Maker, according to the binding tips.
- Or make double bias binding. Cut a bias strip 4" (10 cm) wide by the neckline circumference plus 1" or 2.5 cm (about 31" or 78.5 cm). Trim one end and turn under ½" (1.3 cm). Press. Fold the strip in half lengthwise, wrong sides together. Press.
7. Bind the neckline.
- Pin the strip to the neckline, right sides together, shaping it around the curve. Position the folded end at the center back *(Diagram E)*. Don't stretch or ease the bias too much.

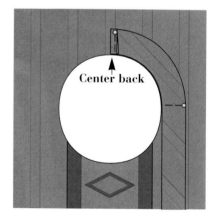

**Diagram E**

- Straightstitch the strip to the neckline, using a ½" (1.3 cm) seam allowance *(Diagram F)*. Lap the raw end of the strip over the folded end about 1" (2.5 cm), and trim any excess.

---

### Tip from Gail

When you're cutting straight lines, such as the rectangles for these cover-ups, save time by using a rotary cutter with a quilting ruler and rotary-cutting mat.

---

- Cut out the cover-up.
2. Form the front pocket/hem.
- Fold the sheet border up on the right side of the fabric; press.
- Edgestitch both short ends of the border *(Diagram B)*.
- Hold up the cover-up to check the length. Make any necessary length adjustments on the unhemmed short end.

**Diagram F**

- Fold the doubled strip over the seam toward the inside, lapping over the stitching line about ⅛" (3 mm). Pin.
- Starting at the center back, stitch-in-the-ditch to secure the binding *(Diagram G)*. See page 135 for how to stitch-in-the-ditch.

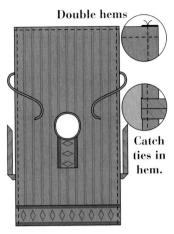

**Diagram G**

8. Stitch bias front ties.
- Fold a 4" x 20" (10 cm x 51 cm) bias strip, right sides together, and stitch the long edges, using a ¼" (6 mm) seam.

- Center the seam and stitch one end diagonally. Trim and layer the seam allowance. Turn right side out.
- Repeat for the second tie.

9. Add finishing details.
- Try on the cover-up, and narrow it as desired, allowing 3" (7.5 cm) for each side hem.
- Pin the ties and ribbons in place on the cover-up.
- Stitch a 1½"-wide (3.8 cm-wide) double hem on each side of the cover-up *(Diagram H)*. See page 135 for how to make a double hem. Be sure to catch the ties in the hem as you sew.

- Topstitch to form pockets as desired in the front hem/pocket.

**Double hems**

Catch ties in hem.

**Diagram H**

# Bonus Project: Child's Cover-up

You can cut a Child's Cover-up from the same twin flat sheet used for the Adult Cover-up. Refer to *Diagram A* on page 20 to cut the child's version. Check to be sure it's wide enough to fit around your child, and then make it just like the adult's, but narrow the side hems to 1" (2.5 cm). Make the front ties the same width as the adult version, then fold them in half and sew them to the sides *(diagram at right)*. What a fun gift for a special helper!

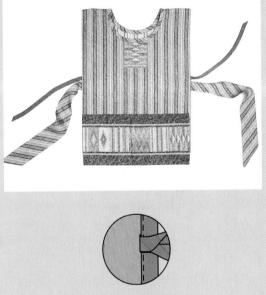

**Fold ties in half before stitching in side hem.**

# From Towels

*At the pool, beach, or bath, these getups add warmth and imaginative fun for any child. The basic ingredients are as simple as the sewing: a bath towel and a matching washcloth. (For bigger kids, see page 24.)*

## Tot's Getup

### Gather Supplies
- 1 bath towel and 1 matching washcloth
- Fabric marking pen
- Fabric scraps for appliqués
- Stitchable, paper-backed fusible web
- Thread to match
- Water-soluble stabilizer
- Tear-away stabilizer
- Pen or pencil, and tracing paper, pattern paper, or waxed paper
- Optional: fusible interfacing

### Create Tot's Getup
Note: Patterns for the cow, bunny, and dog are on pages 139–142.

1. Fold the washcloth approximately in half, right sides together, extending the lower portion 1" (2.5 cm) beyond the upper portion.

2. Shape the upper edge of the hood.
- Pin ¼" (6 mm) seam allowances at the side seams.
- Shape the washcloth for the ears by measuring 2" to 3" (5 cm to 7.5 cm) from both sides of the corners and marking with pins (Diagram A).

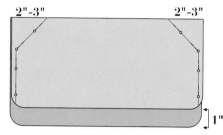

**Diagram A**

- Pin diagonally between the marks, and then mark the line with a fabric marking pen.
- Turn the hood right side out.
3. Prepare appliqués and stitch them to the hood.
- Trace facial features on the paper side of paper-backed fusible web.
- Roughly cut out the shapes.
- Fuse the web to the wrong side of the appliqué fabric.
- Cut out the shapes; remove the paper backing.
- Position appliqués on the hood using pins or tape (Diagram B). See page 128 for how to apply appliqués.

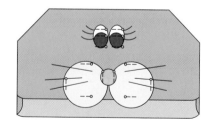

**Diagram B**

- Remove the pins from the side seams so that the washcloth is flat. Cover the appliqués with a press cloth and fuse.
- Satin-stitch around the appliqués.
4. Prepare the ears.

- Trace the desired ear shape onto pattern paper, tracing paper, or waxed paper.
- Use the pattern to cut four ears from appliqué fabric. To add firmness to lightweight fabric, fuse interfacing to the wrong side of the fabric before cutting out the pattern pieces.
- With right sides facing, stitch two ears together along marked lines using a ¼" (6 mm) seam allowance. Repeat for the other ear. For the bunny, add the inner-ear appliqué before stitching the ears together.
- Turn the ears right side out.
- Form a ⅜" (1 cm) tuck at the unsewn edge of each ear. Machine-baste across the bottom.

5. Stitch the hood.
- Refold the washcloth with right sides together, extending the lower edge by 1" (2.5 cm). Pin.
- Cut each corner along the angled line (Diagram C).

**Diagram C**

- Place the ears between the washcloth sections along the angled corners. Make sure the right sides of the ears face the appliquéd hood. Pin.

- Stitch across the angled area and down the sides (Diagram D). Clean-finish the seam edges by zigzagging or serging.

**Diagram D**

- Turn the hood right side out.
6. Make tucks in the upper edge of the towel.
- Fold the towel in half, meeting the short ends. Mark the center point along one edge.
- Measure and fold three 1" (2.5 cm) tucks on each side of the center mark, folding tucks toward the center. Machine-stitch across the tucks (Diagram E).

Center

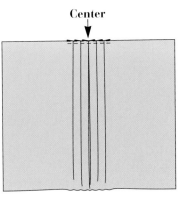

**Diagram E**

7. Appliqué details, such as spots, tails, and feet, on the towel.
8. Overlap the right side of the hood extension with the wrong side of the upper edge of the towel, matching centers. The hood should extend 1" (2.5 cm) past the towel edge. Edgestitch. For added security, stitch a second time, along the edge of the washcloth (Diagram F).

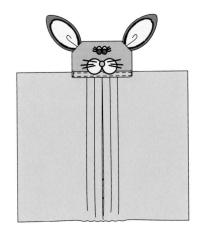

**Diagram F**

# Bonus Project: Super-Quick Wrap

For an even quicker wrap, trim the hood and towel with ribbon instead of appliqués. Edgestitch ribbon along one edge of the hood and along the short ends of the towel.

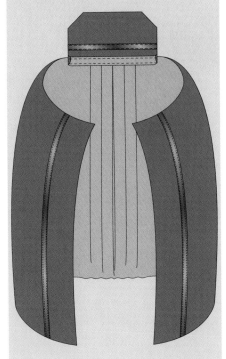

**Diagram A**

*Our Child's Getup looks a lot like the Tot's Getup (page 22), but it's a pullover rather than a wraparound, and you substitute a hand towel for the hood.*

# Child's Getup

## Gather Supplies
- 1 bath towel and 1 matching hand towel
- Fabric scraps for appliqués
- Stitchable, paper-backed fusible web
- Water-soluble stabilizer
- Tear-away stabilizer
- Thread to match
- Optional: Monofilament thread

## Create Child's Getup
1. Trim one lengthwise edge of the hand towel so that the towel measures 14" (35.5 cm) wide *(Diagram A)*.

2. Refer to Step 3 of Tot's Getup (page 22) to prepare and stitch appliqué features along the uncut edges of the hand towel. (Note: For cow face, appliqué the large spot shown in the photo after you shape the hood. Patterns for all features are on pages 139–142.)
3. Shape the upper edge of the hood.
- Fold the hand towel in half with right sides together, meeting the short ends *(Diagram B)*.

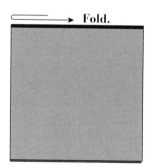

**Diagram B**

- Stitch a ¼" (6 mm) seam along the cut edge of the hand towel. Clean-finish the seam edges by zigzagging or serging.
- Fold the hand towel, wrong side out, so that a triangular point forms and the seam lies in the center of the triangle.
- Measure 5" (12.5 cm) from the point. Trim the upper part of the triangle.

4. Prepare the ears as in Step 4 of Tot's Getup. Pin in place with right sides of the ears toward the face, between the hand towel sections *(Diagram C)*.

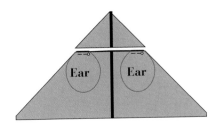

**Diagram C**

5. Sew the hood.
- Stitch a ¼" (6 mm) seam across the top of the hood, catching the base of each ear in the seam. Clean-finish the seam by zigzagging or serging.
- Turn the hood right side out. For cow face, appliqué the large spot as shown in the photograph.
- Measure and fold one 1½" (3.8 cm) tuck on each side of the center back seam on the hood. Machine-baste across both tucks *(Diagram D)*.

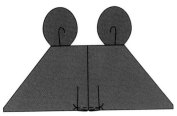

**Diagram D**

6. Complete the cover-up.
- Fold the towel in half, right sides together, with shorter ends meeting. Mark the center fold.
- Open the towel and center the neckline pattern from page 138 over the center fold. Mark the neckline shape on the towel, and cut the neckline opening. Clean-finish the neck opening by zigzagging or serging *(Diagram E)*.

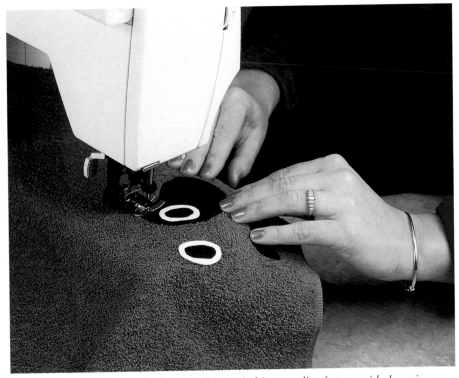

*Use monofilament thread when machine-stitching appliqués to avoid changing thread each time you stitch a different color appliqué.*

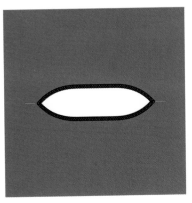

**Diagram E**

7. Appliqué finishing details, such as spots, tails, and feet, on the towel.
8. Attach the hood *(Diagram F)*.
- With right sides together, line up the hood's center back with the center back on the towel neck opening. Pin and stitch in place with a ½" (1.3 cm) seam allowance. Zigzag or serge the raw edges.
- Turn right side out.

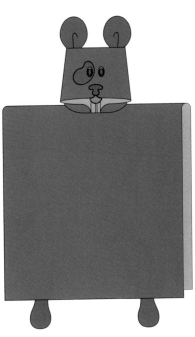

**Diagram F**

Transform a bath towel and a washcloth into a sure-to-be-welcome gift for active family or friends. One short sewing session is all you need to finish this workout towel. Then personalize it with an appliqué or easy embellishment.

# Workout Towel

## Gather Supplies
- 1 large or full-size bath towel and 1 matching washcloth
- Serger thread to match
- Stitchable, paper-backed fusible web
- Optional: Fabric scraps for appliqués
- Optional: Embroidery thread for appliqués

## Create Workout Towel
1. Create the pockets.
- Cut the washcloth in half to create two pockets. If the washcloth has decorative trim along the ends, use those edges as the tops of the pockets.
- Round the lower corners of the pockets *(Diagram A)*, using a cup or a Radial Rule (see *Note from Nancy*, page 98).

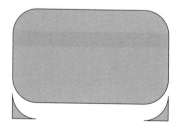

**Diagram A**

- Serge the cut edges with a 3-thread or a 3/4-thread overlock. (See page 132 for serging tips.)
- Optional: Add appliqués to the pockets. (See page 128 for appliqué tips.)

2. Cut the bath towel the width of the pocket.
3. Pin one pocket to each end of the towel. Round the towel ends to match the pockets *(Diagram B)*.

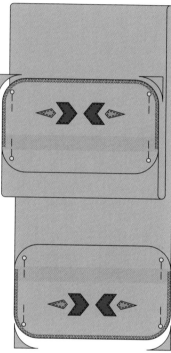

**Diagram B**

4. Finish the towel edges with an overlock stitch or with bias binding.
- To serge the edges, place pins parallel to the seam edge to avoid serging over them.
- Thread the serger with all-purpose serger thread that matches the towel.
- Adjust the serger for a 3/4-thread overlock stitch with the widest possible stitch.

- Release the thread chain from the stitch finger on the presser foot. Place your finger behind the threads, just above the needle eyes, and pull forward to loosen the tension. Pull the thread tails, and the thread chain will slip off the stitch finger, making it easier to start serging at the towel edge *(Diagram C)*.

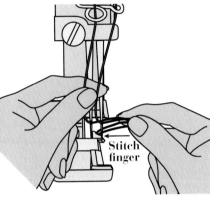

**Diagram C**

- Serge the towel edges, beginning on a single layer and proceeding onto the double layer *(Diagram D)*.

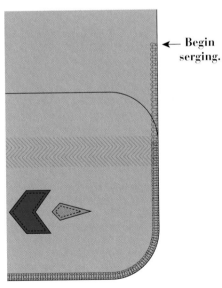

**Diagram D**

- To finish the edges with bias binding *(Diagram E)*, use purchased binding, or make your own using a Bias Tape Maker. See page 130 for how to make and apply binding.

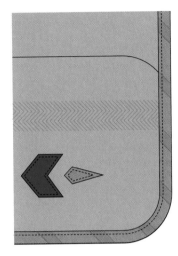

**Diagram E**

5. Divide the washcloth pockets into sections by straightstitching dividers through each pocket and towel. Reinforce stitching at the upper edges of the pocket *(Diagram F)*.

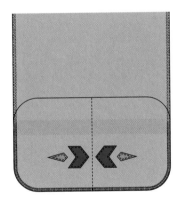

**Diagram F**

# Bonus Project: Golf Towel

My husband Rich and Gail's husband John are avid golfers. As frequent shoppers at pro shops, they've noticed that golf towels are pricey!

You can easily convert a hand towel into a golf towel by hand-sewing a cafe ring to one short end of the towel. Add an appliqué, such as the Southwestern design on the workout towel, or embellish it with your favorite golf-inspired design. A useful gift for golfers!

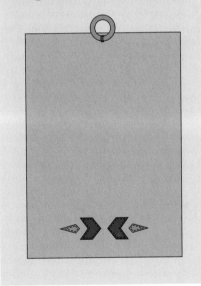

**Diagram**

- With the ribbing on top, straight-stitch ribbing to neckline. Stretch the ribbing slightly to fit.
- Finish the neckline seam with serging or double stitching.
- Lightly steam-press the seam allowance away from the neck-line opening toward the garment.

5. Seam the sides of the poncho. Lap the front over the back ½" (1.3 cm), and straightstitch from the hemline about 14" (35.5 cm).

*Personalize these practical ponchos with monograms, decorative machine stitching, or appliqués, or use an embroidered towel.*

## Pullover Poncho

### Gather Supplies
- 1 bath towel, about 28" x 48" (71 cm x 122 cm)
- 14½" (37 cm) of 2¾"-wide (7 cm-wide) cotton or cotton/polyester ribbing
- Thread to match
- Pencil or pen and paper

### Create Pullover Poncho
1. Transfer the neckline pattern from page 138 onto paper.
2. Fold the towel to mark the center front and the shoulder lines.
3. Cut the neckline opening. Dimensions may vary with differences in towel sizes.
4. Apply neckline ribbing.
- With right sides together, straight-stitch ribbing into a circle. Use ¼" (6 mm) seam allowances through-out unless instructed otherwise. Finger-press the seam open.
- Fold the ribbing in half, wrong sides together. Using long pins, quarter-mark the ribbing.

### Tip from Gail

To quarter-mark ribbing and garment openings, fold instead of measuring. First, fold ribbing or opening in half, and mark the fold lines with long pins (half-marks). Refold, aligning the half-mark pins; use pins to mark the two opposite fold lines. The four pin-marks are quarter-marks.

- Quarter-mark the neckline opening.
- With the ribbing seam at the center back neckline, align the quarter-marks to distribute the neckline ease evenly *(Diagram)*.

## Bonus Project: Baby Bibs

For quick baby gifts, make cute bibs from hand towels, using the same size neckline opening and ribbed finish as the poncho. For extra durability, turn under the side edges about ½" (1.3 cm) and top-stitch twice with a narrow satin stitch.

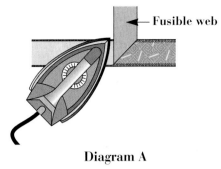

**← Fusible web**

**Diagram A**

6. Fold under the strip ends to fit the towel width. Fuse to the towel, centering the strip to cover the woven-in towel band. Repeat to cover the remaining towel band *(Diagram B)*.

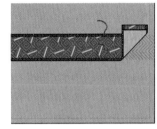

**Diagram B**

7. Edgestitch the fused fabric strips to the towel next to the serged needle lines.

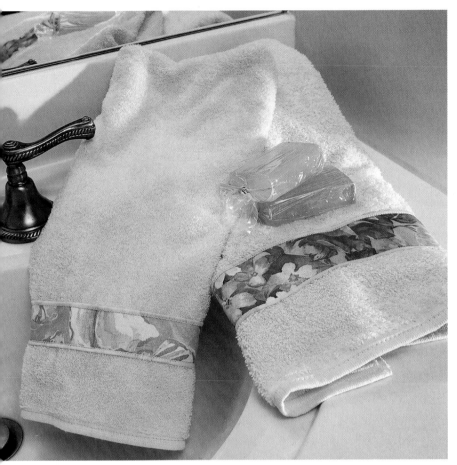

*Transform an everyday essential into a bathroom-boutique specialty. Simply stitch fabric strips to hand and guest towels for an attractive embellishment.*

# Beautiful Borders

## Gather Supplies

- Hand or guest towels
- Serger thread of your choice, for rolled-edge finishing (I recommend a durable, washable, and abrasion-resistant decorative thread for the looper or upper looper, such as Woolly Nylon, Woolly Nylon Extra, Pearl Crown Rayon, or Success Serging Yarn.)
- 38" (96.5 cm) stable, tightly woven decorator fabric or unfinished ribbon. Length may be adjusted; it should be twice towel width plus 2" (5 cm).
- ⅛ yard (0.15 m) stitchable, paper-backed fusible web for each towel
- Thread to match

## Create Beautiful Borders

1. Set up the serger for a narrow rolled-edge stitch. (See page 132 for serging tips.)
2. Cut the fabric into strips at least ½" (1.3 cm) wider than the width of the towel's woven-in bands. (The extra width will be trimmed when you serge.) Lengthwise-grain fabric strips serge-finish more smoothly, with less raveling than crosswise-grain strips.
3. Serge-finish the lengthwise edges of the strip.
4. Cut the serge-finished strips into 18" (46 cm) lengths (or to fit towel plus 1" or 2.5 cm).
5. Fuse paper-backed fusible web to the wrong side of the serge-finished strips and remove the paper layer *(Diagram A)*.

*Tip from Gail*

When serging a rolled edge, try Woolly Nylon in all thread positions. Why? When you use this thread in the needle or the lower looper or both, the strong, resilient fibers resist breaking and enhance tightening. When you use it in the upper looper of a 3-thread stitch or in the looper of a 2-thread stitch, this multifilament thread spreads to cover the edge beautifully.

Always-Right
Accessories

# Classic Scarves

*Making and wearing scarves is fast, fun, and inexpensive. Scarves also make great gifts because they fit and flatter almost everyone.*

## Gather Supplies

- Soft, drapable fabric, such as silk, silklike fabric, lace, chiffon, lightweight wool jersey, or challis (wool or rayon). Add up to ¼ yard (0.25 m) if you plan to finish your scarf edges with self-fabric binding.

**Rectangular scarf:** ⅜ yard (0.35 m) 45"-wide (115 cm-wide) fabric for standard-length scarf
⅜ yard (0.35 m) 60"-wide (150 cm-wide) fabric for long scarf
**Square scarf:** ⅓ yard (0.30 m) 45"-wide (115 cm-wide) fabric to make 3 (10" or 15.5 cm) pocket squares
¾ yard (0.70 m) 45"-wide (115 cm-wide) fabric to make 2 (22" or 56 cm) standard neck squares
1 yard (0.95 m) 45"-wide (115 cm-wide) fabric to make 1 large (36" or 90 cm) square scarf
**Diamond-shaped scarf:** 1⅜ yard (1.30 m) 36"- to 45"-wide (90 cm- to 115 cm-wide) fabric

- Rotary cutter, mat, and quilting ruler
- Thread to match

## Cut Out Scarves

1. Use a rotary cutter, mat, and quilting ruler to cut fabric into squares, rectangles, or other shapes with straight sides.
2. To cut a diamond-shaped scarf:
- Fold the fabric in half lengthwise, and then fold the fabric in half again crosswise, aligning the short ends *(Diagram A)*.

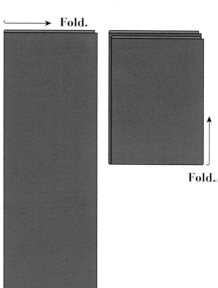

**Diagram A**

- Mark and cut the fabric.
  - •• Place a mark on the cross-wise fold 14" (35.5 cm) from the lengthwise fold.
  - •• Place a mark on the length-wise fold 24" (61 cm) from the crosswise fold *(Diagram B)*.

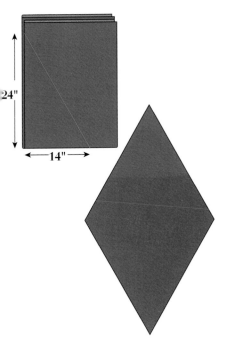

**Diagram B**

•• Draw a line between the two marks and cut along the marked line.

# Scarf Edge Finishes

*Choose clean finishing when you want to add body to scarf edges. No serging, specialty feet, or special stitching are required—only a basic sewing machine.*

## Clean-Finished Edges

### Gather Supplies
- Scarf fabric
- Thread to match

### Create Clean-Finished Edges
1. Stitch ¼" (6 mm) from the fabric edges.
2. Press one edge toward the wrong side of the fabric along the stitching line. Edgestitch into place. Repeat on the opposite edge *(Diagram AA)*.

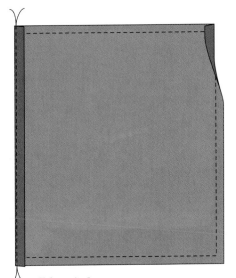

Edgestitch.
**Diagram AA**

3. Repeat for the remaining sides.
4. Beginning with the first edge stitched, fold the pressed edge over again ¼" (6 mm). Press and edgestitch into place, using previous stitching as a guide *(Diagram BB)*. Repeat on the opposite edge and then on the remaining sides.

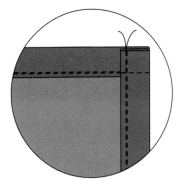

**Diagram BB**

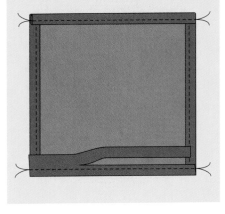

You can bind scarf edges without buying or preparing binding fabric—simply finish with strips of Seams Great®.

## Seams Great Binding

### Gather Supplies
- Scarf fabric
- 1 roll ⅝"-wide (1.5 cm-wide) Seams Great in a color that blends or contrasts with fabric
- Thread to match

### Note from Nancy

Seams Great is a 100% nylon bias-cut tricot sold on a roll and traditionally used as a seam finish. In one easy step, the stretchy nylon curls over a raw edge so that you can sew it in place to finish edges. As a timesaving alternative to cleanfinishing, use the ⅝" (1.5 cm) width to finish scarf edges. This option works well when using solid and print fabrics that coordinate with the basic shades of Seams Great: black, white, or beige.

### Create Seams Great Binding

1. Gently stretch the Seams Great to determine which way it curls.
2. Following the curl direction, wrap the Seams Great over the edge of the scarf, beginning at the center of one side.
3. Using a straightstitch, stitch Seams Great to the fabric edges, gently pulling the tape to curl. Stitch on the Seams Great, not off the edge. Note: If you pull Seams Great too taut, it will pucker (*Diagram A*).

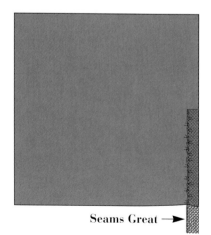

**Seams Great** →

**Diagram A**

4. Miter the binding at the corners.
- Stitch Seams Great to the fabric edge (*Diagram B*). Raise the presser foot and cut the thread tails.

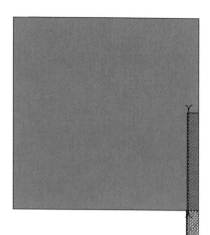

**Diagram B**

- Fold Seams Great around the corner. The previous stitching line will miter the Seams Great.
- Place the fabric/Seams Great under the presser foot and continue stitching, starting at the corner (*Diagram C*). Repeat for other corners.

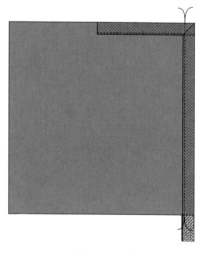

**Diagram C**

5. Overlap the ends of the Seams Great about ½" (1.3 cm). Stitch. Trim the Seams Great close to the stitching.

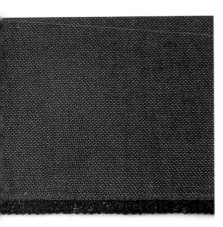

*Lightweight serged edges are common on ready-made scarves. Now, with home-use sergers, you can easily duplicate this look with a narrow rolled-edge finish.*

## Narrow Rolled-Edge Finish

### Gather Supplies
- Scarf fabric
- Specialty thread: 2 to 3 cones Woolly Nylon or 1 spool or cone midweight (not heavy) metallic thread
- Overlock thread to match
- 1 package water-soluble stabilizer

### Create Narrow Rolled-Edge Finish

1. See page 132, to set up your serger for a narrow rolled-edge stitch.
- Option 1 for specialty threads: Use Woolly Nylon in the looper(s) and/or needle position(s).
- Option 2 for specialty threads: Use metallic thread in the upper looper (of a 3-thread stitch) or looper (of a 2-thread stitch).
2. To add stability to scarf edges and to prevent raveling, cut 1" (2.5 cm) strips of water-soluble stabilizer.
3. Serge the scarf edges, stitching over the stabilizer (*Diagram*).

**Serge.**

Stabilizer

**Diagram**

4. Tear or cut away excess stabilizer. Steam or spritz away any remaining traces of stabilizer. Note: Don't spritz fabrics susceptible to water spotting. Always test on a scrap first.

# Bonus Project: Blooming Hankies

Serging streamlines scarf-making. One pocket-scarf style I rely on for my television wardrobe is the "blooming hanky." Using a narrow rolled edge, I serge-finish the edge of a 12" to 13" (30.5 cm to 33 cm) circle of silk, silklike, or lace fabric.

For another quick-and-easy pocket hanky, cut a 4"- to 10"-wide strip of lace galloon (a lace or embroidered trim with scalloped lengthwise edges). Then serge-finish the two cut edges.

*Use a lace galloon (bottom left) or lace yardage (right) to make a Blooming Hanky (top left).*

# Wraps and Shawls

*This pretty scarf requires no knotting or fasteners of any kind, making it less bulky. Instructions are for the muffler version made in popular Polarfleece, but you can also make the scarf in a silk or silklike fabric.*

## Self-Tying Scarf

### Gather Supplies
- ½ yard (0.50 m) Polarfleece or other high-loft fleece
- Thread to match

### Create Self-Tying Scarf
**Note:** All seam allowances are ⅝" (1.5 cm).
1. Cut and mark the fabric.
- Cut two pieces of Polarfleece measuring 40" (102 cm) long. Taper them from 9" (23 cm) wide at one end to 5" (12.5 cm) wide at the other.

- Working from the wrong side, place marks 8½" (22 cm) from the narrow end near the seam edges *(Diagram A)*.

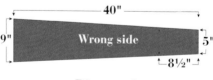

**Diagram A**

2. With right sides together, stitch the narrow ends *(Diagram B)*.

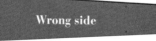

**Diagram B**

3. Clean-finish the neckline area.
- Machine-stitch ⅝" (1.5 cm) from the edge between each mark.
- Clip to the stitching line at each mark.
- Fold the seam allowances to the wrong side between the marks. Topstitch along the fold, using the presser foot as your guide *(Diagram C)*.

**Diagram C**

4. Fold the scarf, right sides together, aligning the 9" (23 cm) ends. Stitch from mark to mark, pivoting at the corners. Grade seam allowances and trim the corners *(Diagram D)*.

**Diagram D**

5. Turn the scarf right side out and press. Topstitch along the edge, using the presser foot as a guide and aligning this stitching with the topstitching in Step 3 *(Diagram E)*.

**Diagram E**

6. To wear the scarf, wrap it around your neck and pull the wide end through the loop *(see photo)*.

*This cozy scarf is a quick gift to serge.*

# Serged Self-Tying Scarf

## Gather Supplies

- ½ yard (0.50 m) Polarfleece or other high-loft fleece
- Overlock thread to match
- Seam sealant

## Create Serged Self-Tying Scarf

1. Set up the serger for a balanced 3- or 3/4-thread overlock stitch, using overlock thread that matches the fabric.
2. Cut and mark the fabric.
- Cut two pieces of Polarfleece measuring 40" (102 cm) long by 8" (20.5 cm) at the wide end and 4" (10 cm) at the narrow end.
- Working from the wrong side, place marks 8½" (22 cm) from the narrow end near the seam edges *(Diagram AA)*.

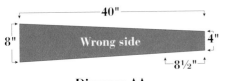

**Diagram AA**

3. With right sides together, serge the narrow ends *(Diagram BB)*.

**Serge.**

**Diagram BB**

4. Serge the neckline area.
- Release the thread chain from the stitch finger. (See page 27.)
- Serge the edges between the marks *(Diagram CC)*.

**Serge.**

**Diagram CC**

5. Fold the scarf, wrong sides together, aligning the 8" (20.5 cm) ends.
6. Serge the outer edges of the scarf together.
- Release the thread chain from the stitch finger.
- Starting at one neckline mark, serge to the first corner, chaining off the corner. Clip the threads.
- Serge the scarf's lower edge, again chaining off the corner.
- Serge the remaining side, starting at the corner and serging to the remaining mark.
- Release the thread chains from the stitch finger at the stopping point. Clip threads *(Diagram DD)*.

**Diagram DD**

- Weave the thread tails under the stitches.
7. To wear the scarf, wrap it around your neck and insert the end through the loop opening *(see photo on page 36)*.

## Note from Nancy

For a lighter scarf, substitute lightweight, drapable, or sheer fabrics. Increase the width of the scarf to 11" (28 cm) at the wide end and 7" (18 cm) at the narrow end.

*This shawl has universal fashion appeal: it's feminine and warm without adding bulk. Cut from a square of fabric, this versatile accessory is considerate of your budget and sewing time.*

# Ruffled Shawl

## Gather Supplies

- Silk or silklike fabric, lace, chiffon, lightweight wool jersey, or rayon or wool challis
  **Small shawl:** 1¼ yards (1.15 m) 45"-wide (115 cm-wide) fabric for 45" (115 cm) shawl
  **Medium shawl:** 1½ yards (1.40 m) 60"-wide (150 cm-wide) fabric for 54" (137 cm) shawl
  **Large shawl:** 1¾ yards (1.60 m) 60"-wide (150 cm-wide) fabric for 60" (150 cm) shawl
- Thread choices depend upon edge-finishing technique. See instructions beginning on page 33 for thread types.
- Tailor's chalk
- Rotary cutter, mat, and ruler

## Create Ruffled Shawl

1. Cut the fabric into the desired size square, using a rotary cutter, mat, and ruler: **small—45"** (115 cm), **medium—54"** (137 cm), **large—60"** (150 cm).
2. Mark and cut the shawl pieces.
- On the wrong side, use tailor's chalk to draw a line between two opposite corners, forming two triangles.
- To cut ruffle pieces, mark one triangle into 3¼"-wide (9 cm-wide) strips *(Diagram A)*.

**Diagram A**

- Cut the fabric along the marked lines, using scissors or a rotary cutter, mat, and ruler.
- To make it easier to stitch the ruffle to the shawl, round the tip of the remaining triangle as illustrated.
3. Prepare the ruffle.
- With right sides together, stitch the ruffle strips into one continuous strip. The ruffle section should measure about twice the length of the shawl's outer edge.
- Taper the short ends of the ruffle.
- Edge-finish the tapered long edge of the ruffle (Diagram B). See pages 33–35 for edge-finishing techniques.

**Diagram B**

4. Edge-finish the scarf long edge.
5. Quarter-mark the unfinished edge of the ruffle and the unfinished scarf edges.
- To quarter-mark the ruffle, fold it in half lengthwise and mark the fold with a pin. Then fold it in half again and mark the two folds with pins. The three pins are the quarter-marks (Diagram C).

**Diagram C**

- To quarter-mark the scarf, place a pin at the point of the triangle as illustrated. Fold the scarf so that the pin meets one corner and mark the fold with a pin; repeat for the other corner (Diagram C).

6. Gather the the long, straight edge of the ruffle. See page 131 for gathering techniques.
7. Stitch the ruffle to the shawl.
- With right sides together, pin the ruffle to the unfinished edges of the shawl, matching the quarter-marks. Align the tapered ends of the ruffle with the points of the shawl.
- Stitch the ruffle section to the shawl, using a ⅝" (1.5 cm) seam allowance.
- Trim the seam allowance and zigzag or serge the raw edges together (Diagram D).

**Diagram D**

# Bonus Project: Basic Head Wraps

People recovering from chemotherapy treatment or having a bad hair day can wear scarves with flair. Folding and twisting a basic 36" (91.5 cm) square scarf yields fun results.

1. Fold a square scarf into a triangle, with one point longer than the other (Diagram AA).

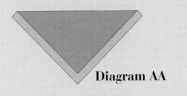

**Diagram AA**

Drape the scarf over your head with the shorter side on top and the points in the back. Tie the ends in a half-knot at the back of the head; roll the point over the knot and tuck in the ends (Diagram BB).

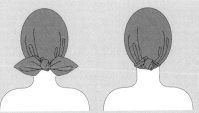

**Diagram BB**

2. Add a contrasting band to the scarf wrap created in option 1. Fold another scarf into a triangle, fold the point to the top fold, and then fold the top fold to align with the bottom fold. Twist (Diagram CC). Place the twisted scarf over the head wrap and tie in the back, tucking in the ends. You can also tie the twisted scarf over one ear and let the tails hang over the shoulder (Diagram DD).

**Diagram CC**

**Diagram DD**

3. To achieve a fuller look, make the basic scarf with fleece and use a silk scarf to sew the contrasting band.

*Gail and Nancy show how this sophisticated wrap can be a great fashion alternative, providing warmth and flair without the weight of a coat. In really cold weather, you can wear it over your coat.*

## Easy, Elegant Wrap

### Gather Supplies

- 2 yards (1.85 m) 54"-wide (140 cm-wide) or wider double-knit, interlock, fleece, or other drapable, ravel-resistant knit
- Thread to match (for conventional finishing) or overlock thread to match (for serged edges)
- Optional: 2.5 mm to 4.0 mm double stretch needle for top-stitching
- Optional: pinking shears for finishing edges, if serger isn't used

### Create Easy, Elegant Wrap

1. Cut out the wrap following the layout shown in *Diagram A*. Finished length, shoulder to hem, is about 33" (84 cm); lengthen or shorten as desired. Finished width is 25" to 30" (63.5 cm to 76 cm); widen or narrow as desired. Before finishing the edges (Steps 2 and 3), try on the wrap and make any necessary length or width adjustments.

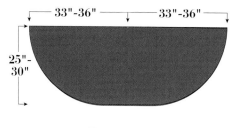

**Diagram A**

2. Finish the wrap edges with serging (instructions on page 132) or pinking.

3. Turn up a ⅝" (1.5 cm) hem along the curved edge. Working from the right side and using a single or double needle, topstitch ½" (1.3 cm) from the hem fold *(Diagram B)*.

**Diagram B**

4. Turn up a ⅝" (1.5 cm) hem along the neckline opening edge, tapering and narrowing to ¼" (6 mm) at the center point *(Diagram C)*. Optional: At the front corners, fold the hem allowance diagonally to miter before topstitching.

**Diagram C**

5. Working from the right side and using a single or double needle, topstitch ½" (1.3 cm) from the hem fold, tapering to ¼" (6 mm) at the center point *(Diagram D)*.

6. Press to smooth the topstitching.

**Diagram D**

# Office Indispensables

Bulletin boards don't have to be strictly utilitarian. You can combine a picture frame with your favorite fabrics to make a charming and functional accessory. For pizzazz, choose a dramatic texture, print, or color contrast.

## Fast Fabric Pinup

### Gather Supplies

- 1 picture frame, 18" x 22" (46 cm x 56 cm) with a 17" x 21" (43 cm x 53.5 cm) opening (If you choose a different size frame, adjust fabric yardages.)
- ¼"-thick (6 mm-thick) foam-core board
- 1¼ yards (1.15 m) lightweight to medium-weight, firmly woven cotton
- Lightweight staple gun and ¼" (6 mm) staples for lightweight fabrics, or ⁵⁄₁₆" (1 cm) staples for medium-weight fabrics
- Optional: 1 or 2 pieces lightweight to medium-weight, firmly woven cotton cut to size of foam-core board (for buffer layer)
- Optional: 2"-wide (5 cm-wide) adhesive tape (for finishing back of bulletin board)
- Optional: Picture-hanging wire and 2 eyebolts, if not provided with frame
- Optional: Glue stick

### Tip from Gail

You can buy foam-core board at most frame or art-supply stores, where they'll often cut it to size for you. Or you can cut it yourself, using a craft knife or a rotary cutter. You can also use corrugated cardboard or even the cardboard that comes with the frame. Just make sure it's sturdy enough to hold the fabric taut without buckling.

### Create Fast Fabric Pinup

1. Remove the cardboard insert and glass from the frame. The insert is your pattern for cutting the foam-core board and the fabric. If a lightweight paper backing board is included, save it for Step 6.
2. Cut the foam-core board the same size as the cardboard insert.
3. Cut the fabric 6" (15 cm) wider and 6" (15 cm) longer than the foam-core board *(Diagram AA)*. Choose any grain as shown.

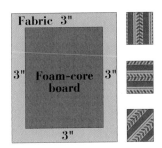

**Diagram AA**

4. Optional: For a buffer layer(s), cut one or two layers of fabric the same size as the cardboard insert. Use a glue stick to secure the padding to the foam-core board.

*(Continued on page 42)*

5. Staple the fabric to the foam-core board *(Diagram BB)*.

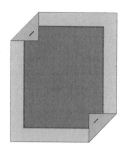

**Diagram BB**

- Center the foam-core board on the wrong side of the fabric with the buffer fabrics (if used) sandwiched in between.
- Working from side to side, pull the fabric taut, smoothing out wrinkles on the right side, and staple it to the foam-core board.

6. Optional: Finish the back of the fabric-covered insert.
- Cover the fabric edges with wide adhesive tape.
- Staple as necessary to secure the layers *(Diagram CC)*.
- Cover the back of the insert with the paper backing board saved from the frame; tape and staple in place *(Diagram DD)*.

7. Place the fabric-covered insert inside the frame. Bend down the staples to hold the insert in place. (Or use hardware provided with the frame to secure the insert.)

8. Optional: Add eyebolts and wires for hanging, if not provided with the frame.

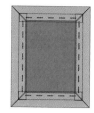

**Diagram CC**

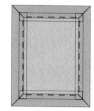

**Diagram DD**

# Bonus Project: Button Tacks

Gail wanted the pins for her Fast Fabric Pinup to be as interesting as the board itself—so she created Button Tacks. Using serrated-tip pliers, she bent a basic dressmaker pin, and then placed the bent end in the shank of a button. The fit was surprisingly snug, requiring no glue! If you can't find shank buttons you like, glue shankless buttons to tacks or pushpins. Whichever method you use, you'll love the look and handling ease of these customized button pins.

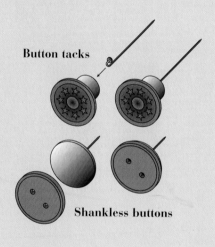

Button tacks

Shankless buttons

## Pocketed Patchwork Pinup

### Gather Supplies

Refer to Fast Fabric Pinup (page 41) for supplies, with the following exceptions and additions:
- No buffer fabric is required.
- Lightweight to medium-weight firmly woven fabric in amounts listed below. Note: Heavier, textured, or loosely woven fabrics are too bulky for layering and too unstable for pocket edges.
    Color A: 1⅓ yards (1.20 m)
    Color B: 1⅞ yards (1.75 m)
    Color C: 1½ yards (1.40 m)
    Color D: ⅝ yard (0.60 m)
    Color E: ⅓ yard. (0.30 m)
Note: Yardages given are for 18" x 22" (46 cm x 56 cm) frame; increase or decrease yardages with frame size.

### Create Pocketed Patchwork Pinup

1. Follow Steps 1, 2, 3, and 5 of Fast Fabric Pinup. Use fabric Color A for Step 3.

Simply fold and staple to create the patchwork pockets of this bulletin board. Customize your color choices as desired: Alternate colors side to side, as shown in the photo, or create a symmetrical design, as illustrated and described in the instructions.

2. Fold and staple fabric to create the patchwork. Always lap the right strips over the left strips. Each exposed strip should measure about 2½" (6.3 cm) wide when finished (or any consistent width throughout).

- Cut two 32" (81.5 cm) squares from Color B. Fold each square in half, wrong sides together. Position the pieces across the insert as shown (Diagram A), with the fabric raw edges to the outside. Use long pins to secure the pieces temporarily, starting on the left side and then pinning the right side in place.

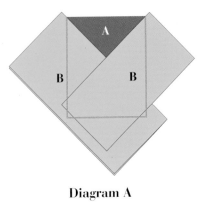

**Diagram A**

- Repeat for Color C, cutting 27" (68.5 cm) squares.

- Repeat for Color D, cutting 22" (56 mm) squares.
- Repeat for Color E, cutting 16" (40.5 cm) squares.
- Repeat for Color A, cutting 11" (28 cm) squares (Diagram B).

**Diagram B**

3. Staple the fabric strips to the insert. Make sure the strips are securely pinned, so that stapling won't distort the size or placement of the strips.
- Use the frame to hold the fabric layers in place temporarily.
- Trim all layers to a 3"-wide (7.5 cm-wide) allowance around the foam-core board (Diagram C). Trim and grade layers to reduce bulk.

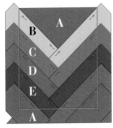

**Diagram C**

- Working side to side, pull the fabric strips taut, smoothing out all wrinkles, and staple them to the insert. Trim and grade bulky fabric areas sandwiched between the outermost fabric and the back of the insert.
4. To complete the bulletin board, follow Steps 6–8 of Fast Fabric Pinup.

# Sewing Specialties

*Use our easy machine-sewn silk-ribbon embroidery to embellish these lovely cases for notions storage. If time is short, omit the embellishment. Pictured (clockwise from top) are the needle case, pin holder, and scissors case.*

## Floral Needle Case

### Gather Supplies

- ¼ yard (0.25 m) or remnants medium-weight fabric
- Fleece remnants
- ¼ yard (0.25 m) fusible interfacing
- Air-soluble fabric marking pen

### Create Floral Needle Case

1. Using the needle case pattern on page 137, cut two layers of fabric, two layers of interfacing, and one layer of fleece. Using the fabric marking pen, outline the embroidery design on the right side of one fabric layer.

2. Fuse interfacing to the wrong side of the fabric *(Diagram A)*.

3. Follow the instructions beginning on page 46 to stitch silk-ribbon embroidery.

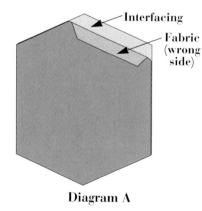

**Diagram A**

4. Stack the sections in this order: fleece; plain fabric, right side up; embroidered fabric, wrong side up *(Diagram B)*.

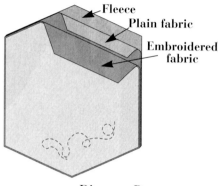

**Diagram B**

5. Stitch a ¼" (6 mm) seam along one edge. Grade and press.

6. Wrap each corner by folding the seam allowance along the stitching line toward the center of the case. Stitch the adjacent seam, starting at the fold *(Diagram C)*. Grade the seam allowance and trim the corner.

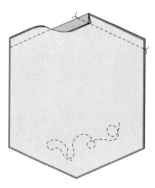

**Diagram C**

7. Stitch the remaining seams, wrapping the corners. Leave an opening for turning *(Diagram D)*. Grade seams and angle-cut corners.

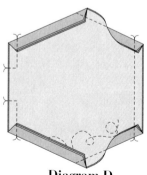

**Diagram D**

8. Turn the case right side out. Transfer the pattern stitching lines to the case, and machine-stitch along the marked lines *(Diagram E)*.

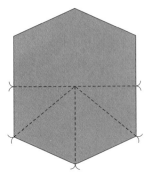

**Diagram E**

9. Add ribbon ties on the case front.

# Floral Scissors Case

## Gather Supplies
- ¼ yard (0.25 m) or remnants medium-weight fabric
- ¼ yard (0.25 m) or remnants fusible interfacing
- Fleece remnants
- Air-soluble fabric marking pen

## Create Floral Scissors Case
1. Using the scissors case pattern on page 137, cut two fronts and two backs from fabric and from interfacing. Cut one each from fleece. Use the fabric marking pen to outline the embroidery design on the right side of one of the front fabric layers.
2. Fuse interfacing to the wrong side of the fabric sections.
3. Follow the instructions beginning on page 46 to stitch silk-ribbon embroidery, according to the outlined design.
4. Stitch the case front.
- Make a fabric sandwich, stacking the sections in this order: fleece; plain fabric, right side up; embroidered fabric, wrong side up.

- With right sides facing, stitch the straight edge; press *(Diagram AA)*.

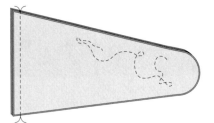

**Diagram AA**

- Wrap the seam allowances toward the center of the case along the stitching line. Stitch the curved edges, leaving an opening for turning *(Diagram BB)*.

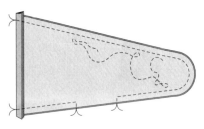

**Diagram BB**

- Turn the case front right side out; press. Stitch the opening closed.
5. Repeat Step 4 to stitch the scissors case back.
6. With wrong sides together, whipstitch the case front and the case back, leaving the top open.
7. Fold the flap down along the fold line indicated on the pattern *(Diagram CC)*. Press.

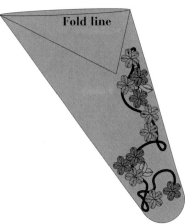

**Diagram CC**

# Floral Pin Holder

## Gather Supplies
- Medium-weight fabric remnants
- Interfacing remnants
- Fleece remnants
- Lightweight cardboard
- Air-soluble fabric marking pen

## Create Floral Pin Holder
1. Using the pin holder pattern on page 137, cut two layers of fabric, two layers of interfacing, two layers of cardboard, and one layer of fleece. Outline the embroidery design on the right side of one fabric layer.
2. Fuse interfacing to the wrong side of the fabric sections.
3. Follow the instructions beginning on page 46 to stitch silk-ribbon embroidery.
4. Center the fleece circle on the wrong side of the embroidered fabric circle and top with a cardboard circle.
5. Fold fabric edges to the wrong side of the circle, around the edges of the cardboard *(Diagram)*. Clip outer edges as needed and overlap clipped sections to achieve a smooth curve. Glue or fuse edges in place.

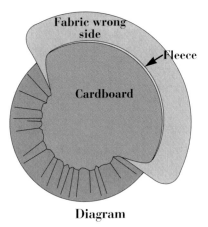

**Diagram**

6. Repeat Steps 4 and 5 without the fleece to make a second fabric-covered circle.
7. With wrong sides facing, glue or stitch the circles together.
8. Insert pins around outer edge of the pin holder *(see photo, page 44)*.

# Silk-Ribbon Embroidery Made Simple

*Note from Nancy*

When embellishing small fabric pieces, Gail and I like to use stabilizer to increase the fabric size. The stabilizer fits in the hoop and securely positions the fabric for silk-ribbon embroidery.

*Preparing your machine for silk-ribbon embroidery is easy. Set up an embroidery hoop, select ribbon, adjust the machine, and you're ready to embroider.*

## Setup for Silk-Ribbon Embroidery

### Gather Supplies
- 2 mm- and 4 mm-wide silk ribbon
- 5" (12.5 cm) or 8" (20.5 cm) wooden or spring-tension machine embroidery hoop
- 1 package stabilizer, such as Avalon® Soluble, Stitch & Ditch, Totally Stable Iron On, or stabilizer of your choice
- Monofilament thread for needle
- Thread to match for bobbin
- Metafil needle for preventing skipped stitches and fraying thread
- Optional: stiletto for positioning ribbon while stitching
- Optional: diamond eye needle for pulling ribbon to wrong side of fabric

### Prepare for Embroidery
1. Cut a square of stabilizer several inches larger than the hoop. Outline embroidery design on the fabric and place it in the center of the stabilizer. Machine-baste around fabric edges, or if using iron-on stabilizer, press the fabric in place *(Diagram A)*.

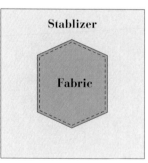

**Diagram A**

2. Separate the hoop pieces and place the stablized fabric over the large piece of the hoop *(Diagram B)*. Insert the remaining hoop section, making sure that the fabric is taut.

**Diagram B**

3. Adjust the sewing machine.
- Insert a Metafil needle *(Diagram C)*.

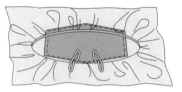

**Elongated eye**

**Diagram C**

- Thread the top of the machine with monofilament thread.
- Thread the bobbin with thread that matches the fabric.
- Remove the presser foot and lower the feed dogs.
- Reduce (loosen) the top tension by two numbers or notches.
- Set the machine to straightstitch. Stitch length is not important because you control it by moving the hoop.
- If possible, adjust the machine so that it stops with the needle in the down position.

- Get ready to sew.
- Place the hooped fabric under the needle.
- Hold the top thread, turning the fly wheel by hand to take one stitch. When the bobbin thread loops over the top thread, pull the bobbin thread to the fabric surface (Diagram D).

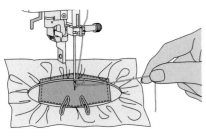

**Diagram D**

- Lower the presser bar (Diagram E). **Important:** Lowering the presser bar engages the top tension and prevents a tangled mass of thread from accumulating on the wrong side of the fabric.

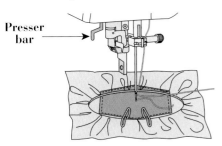

Presser bar

**Diagram E**

- Hold both threads. Stitch in place two or three stitches. Stop with the needle down, in the fabric.
- Clip the thread tails (Diagram F).

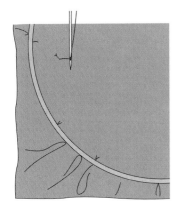

**Diagram F**

# Basic Silk-Ribbon Machine Stitches

Stitching silk-ribbon embroidery by machine involves two basic stitches: the tackstitch and the walkstitch. It's amazing how many stitch variations and interesting designs you can create merely by combining and modifying these basic stitches.

## Tackstitch

1. Place the ribbon on the fabric at the desired position.
2. Stitch back and forth across the ribbon several times to attach it (Diagram AA).

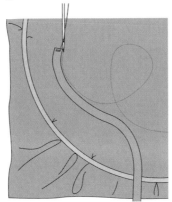

**Diagram AA**

## Walkstitch

1. Position the ribbon on the fabric.
2. Stitch along the side of the ribbon without catching the ribbon, moving the hoop as you stitch, or "walk," to the next tack point (Diagram BB).

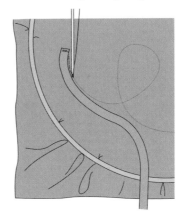

**Diagram BB**

## Twisted Ribbon Stitch

Use this stitch for background stems, outlines, and straight or curved lines.

1. Use 2 mm-wide ribbon. (Narrow ribbon produces more graceful twists.) Cut the ribbon two to two and one-half times the length of the traced design line.
2. Tackstitch the center of the ribbon to the fabric.
3. Twist the two ribbons together by hand. If you want to create loops, twist the ribbon very tightly.
4. Walkstitch, positioning the ribbon along the marked design line (Diagram CC). Tackstitch the ribbon to the traced line approximately every ½" (1.3 cm) (Diagram DD).

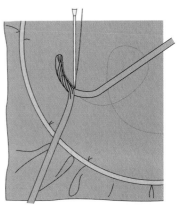

**Diagram CC**

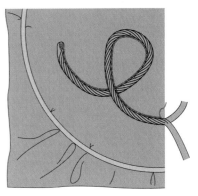

**Diagram DD**

5. When stitching curved lines, walkstitch along the inside of the curve. This makes it easier to mold the twisted ribbon around the needle for a smoother shape or design.

(Continued on page 48)

## Lazy Daisy Stitch

We used this versatile stitch to create leaves in our design on page 46, but you can also use it to make flower petals *(Diagram A)*.

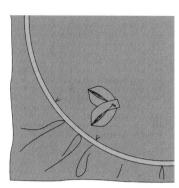

**Diagram A**

1. Use 4 mm-wide ribbon.
2. Tackstitch the ribbon to the fabric at the base of the leaf.
3. Walkstitch to the leaf point about ½" (1.3 cm) away, stopping with the needle in the fabric *(Diagram B)*.

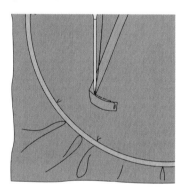

**Diagram B**

4. Wrap the ribbon around the back of the needle, holding the ribbon gently rather than pulling it taut *(Diagram C)*. Tackstitch.

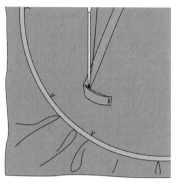

**Diagram C**

5. Walkstitch back to the base of the leaf. Place the ribbon in front of the needle at the leaf base *(Diagram D)*. Tackstitch.

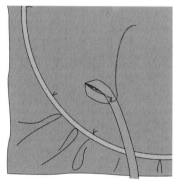

**Diagram D**

6. Angle the hoop slightly and stitch two or three more leaves *(Diagram E)*. At the end of the final leaf, tackstitch again.

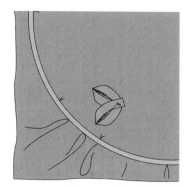

**Diagram E**

7. Finish the leaf in one of the following ways:
- If the leaf end will be covered with other embroidery, trim the ribbon close to the stitching.
- If the leaf end will be exposed, cut the ribbon, leaving a thread tail. Use a diamond eye needle to pull the ribbon to the wrong side of the fabric *(Diagram F)*.

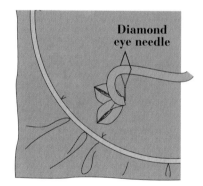

**Diagram F**

# Knotted Ribbon Stitch

This stitch makes a pretty single flower *(Diagram G)*. Use it to make flower clusters that resemble violets or forget-me-nots.

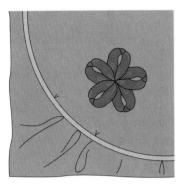

**Diagram G**

1. Select three different shades of one color of 4 mm-wide silk ribbon. Cut multiple 8"-long (20.5 cm-long) strands of each color.

*Note from Nancy*

Varying the ribbon color adds dimension to the flower cluster. Use shades of purple for violets and shades of pink for forget-me-nots.

2. Gently knot each ribbon strand five times, spacing the knots ¾" (2 cm) apart. Leave the last segment (¾" or 2 cm) of the ribbon unknotted *(Diagram H)*.

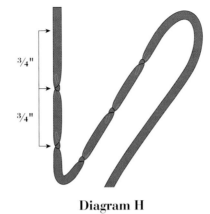

¾"

¾"

**Diagram H**

3. Stitch a flower.
- Tackstitch the ribbon end to the project (a).
- Fold the ribbon at the first knot (b), and then loop the ribbon back to the tack point.
- Tackstitch the ribbon to the fabric (a), tacking between the first and second knots *(Diagram I)*.

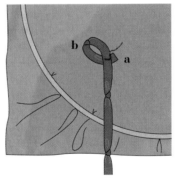

**Diagram I**

- Trim any excess thread tail at the tacked end of the ribbon.
- Fold the ribbon back to the center at the second knot *(Diagram J)*. Place the midpoint between the two knots over the stitched area (c).

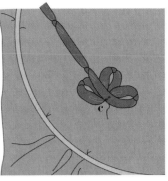

**Diagram J**

- Tackstitch.
- Repeat until you have folded all knots and stitched all midpoints in place.
4. Fold the ribbon tail under and tackstitch. Trim excess thread tails.
5. Add more clusters of folded ribbon.

*Note from Nancy*

I often use a stiletto to help position and control the silk ribbon so it's less likely to twist and tangle as I stitch. The stiletto also keeps my fingers away from the needle area, so that I don't become part of the design!

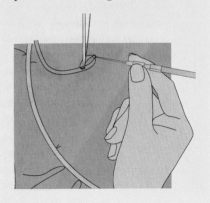

# Basic Pillows

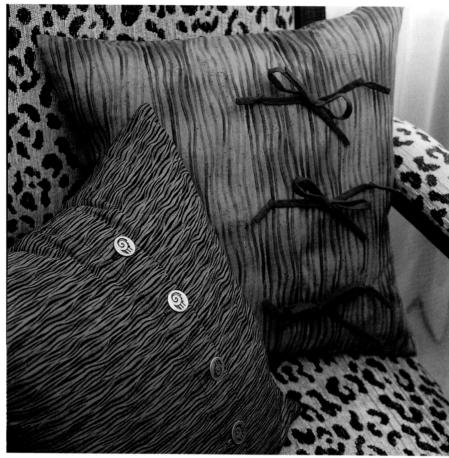

*Whether placed on a sofa or on the floor, these pillows soften surfaces and interior angles, while providing lush color and textural contrast. Use unusual buttons (left) or ties to make the closure part of the pillow's design.*

## Basic Pillow

### Gather Supplies

Note: Unless specified otherwise, fabric yardages given in this chapter are based on 45"-wide (115 cm-wide) fabric.

- ¾ yard to 1⅛ yards (0.70 m to 1.05 m) pattern paper
- ½ yard (0.50 m) medium-weight fabric for 12" to 16" (30.5 cm to 40.5 cm) square pillow, or 1¼ yards (1.15 m) medium-weight fabric for 18" to 20" (46 cm to 51 cm) square pillow
- ⅛ yard (0.15 m) or remnants fusible interfacing (for stabilizing closure sections)
- Fabric marking pen or pencil

- Square pillow form, 12" to 20" (30.5 cm to 51 cm) as desired
- 5 (¾" or 2 cm) buttons
- Optional: 15" to 21" (38 cm to 53.5 cm) Space-Tape™
- Optional: 1 yard of 1"-wide (0.95 m of 2.5 cm-wide) fabric strips for ties
- Optional: 10" (25.5 cm) length of Velcro® or Snap Tape

### Create Basic Pillow

1. Make a pattern.
- Cut a square out of the pattern paper, the size of the pillow form plus 1½" (3.8 cm).
- Fold the square in half, aligning opposite sides; cut along the fold, making two half pieces.

- Use one half as the pillow top pattern. Mark a fold line along one long edge and place nips at both ends of the fold.
- Use the second half as the pattern for the pillow closure. Add a 4½" (11.5 cm) extension along one long edge, and place nips 3" (7.5 cm) and 4½" (11.5 cm) from the edge. Mark the pattern "Cut 2" *(Diagram A)*.

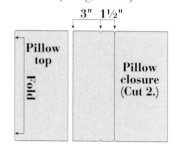

**Diagram A**

2. Cut out the pattern.
- Fold the fabric in half, wrong sides together, aligning selvages.
- Place the pillow top pattern on the fabric, aligning the pattern fold line with the fabric fold. Pin.
- Place the pillow closure pattern on the fabric, with the short edges parallel to the selvages. Pin *(Diagram B)*.

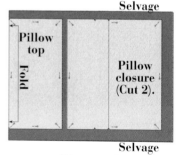

**Diagram B**

- Cut out the pattern pieces.
3. Mark the fabric with ¼" (6 mm) nips at the fold of the pillow top and at the marked positions on the pillow closure side.
4. Interface the hem edge of the closure sections. (See page 129 for interfacing tips.)
- Cut two rectangles of interfacing 3" (7.5 cm) wide by the length of the pattern pieces.

- Place the interfacing pieces on the wrong side of each closure section (Diagram C).

**Diagram C**

- Fuse interfacing in place following manufacturer's instructions.

5. Prepare the closure hems.

- Fold under a hem on each closure piece. If the fabric is prone to raveling, zigzag or serge the interfaced hem edge, or fold under the edge ¼" (6 mm) and stitch. With wrong sides together, fold and press each closure piece along the first nip marking, creating a hem (Diagram D).

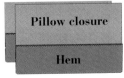

**Diagram D**

- Overlap the two closure pieces, matching the second set of nips, forming a square. Pin the overlap (Diagram E).

**Diagram E**

6. Add a closure in one of the following ways:

**Button Closure:**

- Mark a line on the overlap, joining the second set of nip marks.
- Determine the number of buttonholes, spacing them approximately 3" (7.5 cm) apart.

- Stitch buttonholes along the marked center line (Diagram F).

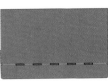

**Diagram F**

- Stitch buttons under the buttonholes along the center line of the underlay.

## Note from Nancy

To make stitching buttonholes even easier, try Space-Tape (see photo below). This see-through tape is printed with colored horizontal and vertical markings that help you stitch buttonholes ranging from ½" to 1" (1.3 cm to 2.5 cm) long. Stick adhesive-backed Space-Tape on the pillow, and stitch the buttonholes over the tape. Tear away excess tape, and you're finished!

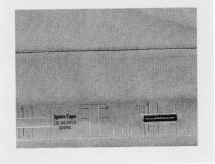

**Tie Closure:**

- Cut two 12" (30.5 cm) lengths of trim, such as cording, leather strips, or fabric tubes. (See page 135 for making fabric tubes.)
- Tie a knot 1" (2.5 cm) from each trim end.
- Stitch one tie to the center of the overlap, sewing next to the knot.
- Stitch a second tie to the underlay, positioning it 3" (7.5 cm) from the overlap tie.

**Velcro or Snap Tape Closure:**

- Cut a 10" (25.5 cm) length of Velcro or Snap Tape
- Center the strip of hook-and-loop or snap tape under the overlap. Offset one long edge of the tape slightly from the fold. Use a fabric marking pen or pencil to mark the position of the set on the overlap and the underlay.
- Separate the two closure pieces. Position the hook section at the marked position on the overlap and the loop section at the marked position on the underlay. Straightstitch. (To prevent cut edges of Snap Tape from raveling, turn under short ends before stitching.)

7. Stitch the pillow sections together.

- Overlap the closure sections, matching the nips. Align the pillow top and pillow closure sections, right sides together. Pin.
- Stitch the upper and lower edges with ⅝" (1.5 cm) seams.
- Press the seam allowances flat; then fold the seams toward the pillow center along the stitching lines and press again (Diagram G). This wraps the seam allowances and makes it easier to produce sharp corners and crisp edges.

Wrap corners.

**Diagram G**

- Stitch the remaining two seams, sewing from fold to fold and creating a wrapped corner.
- Cut the corners at an angle.
- Turn the pillow cover right side out, press, and insert pillow form.

## Create Exposed-Cording Pillow

1. Make a pattern and cut out the pillow, following Steps 1–3 of Basic Pillow.
2. Cut the loop strips into 3"-long (7.5 cm-long) sections. With wrong sides together, fold the sections in half, creating 1½"-long (3.7 cm-long) loops *(Diagram A)*.

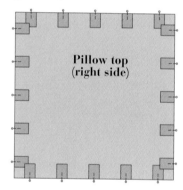

**Diagram A**

3. Pin the loops to the right side of the pillow top, aligning the cut edges and spacing the loops 2" to 3" (5 cm to 7.5 cm) apart *(Diagram B)*.

**Diagram B**

4. Finish the pillow as detailed in Basic Pillow, Steps 4–7.
5. Turn the pillow cover right side out and thread cording through the loops, adjusting to fit. Tie the cording ends together *(Diagram C)*.

**Diagram C**

*Cord the pillow edge without the time-consuming task of covering cording and sewing it into the seam. Our cording is exposed and easily adjusted to fit, peeking in and out of fabric loops.*

# Exposed-Cording Pillow

## Gather Supplies

Refer to Basic Pillow, page 52, with the following additions:
- 1"-wide (2.5 cm-wide) synthetic leather or suede strips, or 2"-wide (5 cm-wide) coordinating fabric strips
- Drapery cord to measure the perimeter of the pillow plus 6" (15 cm)

### *Note from Nancy*

Synthetic leather or suede doesn't ravel, so you won't need to finish the edges of the strips. However, if you use fabric that ravels, cut strips 2" (5 cm) wide. Press the long edges to the center and topstitch allowances in place.

Topstitch.

Topstitch.

# Window Pillows

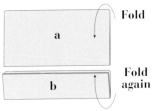

- Cut the fabric for the facing the size of the folded paper (one-fourth the base pillow).
- Unfold the paper pattern so that three of the four sections are visible. Cut the clear vinyl from that portion (*Diagram BB*).

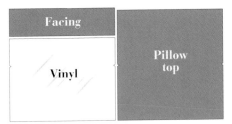

**Diagram BB**

4. Sew the facing to the pillow top.
- Press under ¼" (6 mm) on one long edge of the facing. Place the facing on the pillow top, aligning the cut edges.
- Edgestitch the facing to the pillow top along the fold (*Diagram CC*).

**Diagram CC**

*Showcase pictures or store found objects in this unique pillow. Clear vinyl provides the window for your treasures.*

- Trim pillow top fabric behind the facing.
- Select a zipper longer than the pillow. Apply Basting Tape to the wrong side of the zipper tape along both edges. Peel the paper covering from one edge.

*(Continued on page 56)*

## Basic Window Pillow

### Gather Supplies
Refer to Basic Pillow, page 52, with the following additions:
- ¼ yard (0.25 m) coordinating fabric for window
- ½ yard (0.50 m) clear vinyl
- 22" (55 cm) zipper
- Basting Tape

## Create Basic Window Pillow

1. Make a pattern and cut it out, following Steps 1–3 for Basic Pillow.
2. Stitch the closure side as for Basic Pillow, Steps 4–6.
3. Make the window pattern and cut out fabric and vinyl.
- Cut a paper square the size of the pillow form plus 1½" (3.8 cm).
- Fold the square in half to crease (a in *Diagram AA*). Fold in half again and crease (b).

- Place one long edge of the vinyl over the exposed Basting Tape, ⅛" (3 mm) from the zipper teeth. Finger-press. (The zipper end extends past the vinyl.)
- Stitch over the end of the zipper several times ¼" (6 mm) from the edge of the vinyl. Cut the zipper tape even with the vinyl.
- Stitch along the edge of the zipper tape, joining the zipper to the vinyl *(Diagram DD)*.

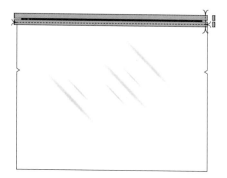

**Diagram DD**

- Place the vinyl/zipper section over the pillow top, aligning the cut edges. Remove remaining paper backing from the Basting Tape. Finger-press the zipper to the pillow top.
- Topstitch the second side of the zipper to the pillow top *(Diagram EE)*.

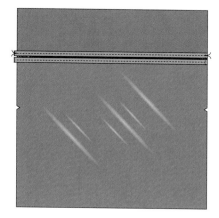

**Diagram EE**

5. Complete the pillow as detailed in Steps 6 and 7 of Basic Pillow, opening the zipper to the center to prevent stitching over the tab.

*You can duplicate a cherished photo on fabric and frame it with fabric strips. Guaranteed: It will be your most talked-about and timeless pillow design.*

# Picture Frame Pillow

## Gather Supplies
Refer to Basic Pillow, page 52, with the following changes:
- ⅜ yard to ⅝ yard (0.35 m to 0.60 m) muslin for pillow top
- ¼ yard (0.25 m) premium-grade muslin for photo transfer
- ⅛ yard to ¼ yard (0.15 m to 0.25 m) each of three different lightweight to medium-weight fabrics
- ½ yard to ⅝ yard (0.50 m to 0.60 m) of a fourth color fabric (for pillow closure side)
- Photo
- Photo transfer paper

## Create Picture Frame Pillow
1. Cut the fabric.
- Cut out the pillow top from regular muslin, following Steps 1–3 of Basic Pillow.
- Cut a piece of premium-grade muslin ½" (1.3 cm) larger on all sides than the photo.

*Note from Nancy*

I recommend using premium-grade muslin for photo transfers. This high-quality fabric has a smooth surface that prevents flecks from marring the completed photo transfer.

- Cut two 2"-wide (5 cm-wide) strips from colors A, B, and C. Cut three 2"-wide (5 cm-wide) strips from color D. Cut the pillow closure side from Color D.

2. Copy the photo on muslin, using instructions on the photo transfer paper package.

3. Use a fabric marking pen to draw lines ¼" (6 mm) from the photo edges. Trim along marked lines.

4. Build the pillow top.

- Baste fabric photo to the center of the muslin pillow top.
- Place a strip of color A along one short end of the photo fabric, right sides together, aligning the edge of the strip and the edge of the trimmed photo fabric. Stitch, using ¼" (6 mm) seams throughout. Trim the remaining strip, being careful not to cut the muslin base. Press the seam flat and then toward strip. Repeat for opposite side *(Diagram A)*.

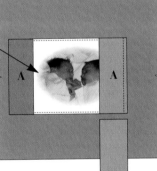

**Diagram A**

- Place strips of color D along the top and bottom of the photo fabric, and stitch as before *(Diagram B)*.

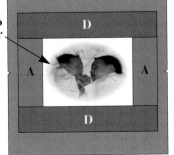

**Diagram B**

- For the second layer, add strips of color B to the ends, and strips of color A to top and bottom.
- For the third layer, add strips of color D to the ends, and strips of color C to top and bottom.
- Repeat adding layers of strips until you cover the muslin base. Trim the pieced top even with the muslin base.

5. Complete the pillow as detailed in Basic Pillow, Steps 4–7.

5. Complete the pillow as detailed in Basic Pillow, Steps 4–7.

## *Note from Nancy*

For a different look, use a fabric print, motif, or embroidery in the center of the pillow top, rather than a photo transfer. Just center and baste the design in place on a muslin base and build the pillow top around your print.

Narrow or widen the fabric strips, or use strips of the same color. You're the designer!

# Bonus Project: Wish Pillow

It's easy to make a Wish Pillow for a favorite child on your gift list. Cut a second pillow front from contrasting or coordinating fabric and fold it in half, wrong sides together. Pin the folded fabric to the right side of the pillow top before sewing the side seams. Within minutes, you'll create a pillow with a pocket—a perfect place to store "wishes!"

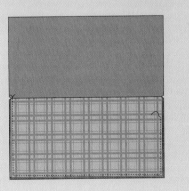

# Easy Diagonal Pillows

To save time and fabric, cut out and sew this pillow style in pairs. The yardage for two is about the same as the yardage for one. The mitered seam results in an eye-catching look.

## Striped Diagonal Pillows

### Gather Supplies

Instructions are for two pillows. Refer to Basic Pillow, page 52, with the following additions:
- Substitute striped fabric.
- Double the fabric amount listed.

### Create Striped Diagonal Pillows

1. Create the pillow front pattern.
- Cut a square paper pattern for the front the size of the pillow form plus 1½" (3.8 cm).
- Fold the paper in half diagonally. Add a ⅝" (1.5 cm) seam allowance along the diagonal fold.
- On the pillow front pattern, mark a grain line parallel to one of the straight cut edges. Write "Cut 2" on the pattern (Diagram A).

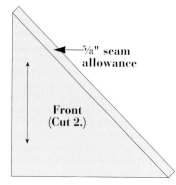

**Diagram A**

2. Cut out the pillow pieces.
- Cut two pillow closure sides from the fabric and prepare them, following Basic Pillow instructions, Steps 1–6.
- Fold the remaining fabric in half, aligning the short ends; match the stripes, pinning if necessary.
- Cut out one set of pillow fronts (Diagram B). Remove the pattern and pin the diagonal edges of the pillow top together.

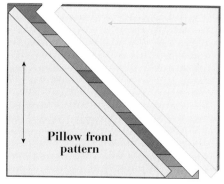

**Diagram B**

- Cut a second pillow front from the remaining fabric. (You have enough yardage to create two pillow fronts.) Pin these pieces together along the diagonal edge.

3. With right sides together, stitch along the diagonal seam using a ⅝" (1.5 cm) seam allowance. Repeat for the second pillow front. Turn pillow fronts right side out and make certain that the stripes match (Diagram C). Press.

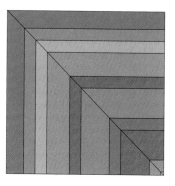

**Diagram C**

4. Refer to Basic Pillow, Step 7, to complete the pillow.

Create strips with patchwork customized in color and texture to coordinate with your decor.

# Diagonal Patchwork Pillow

## Gather Supplies
Refer to Striped Diagonal Pillows, page 58, with the following additions:
- Choose several fabric remnants that coordinate with the pillow fabric
- Rotary cutter, mat, and ruler

## Create Diagonal Patchwork Pillow
1. To create the pillow front pattern, follow Step 1 of Striped Diagonal Pillows.
2. Cut fabric strips.

- Vary the width of the strips between 1½" and 3" (3.8 cm and 7.5 cm) wide, and cut the length at least twice the width of the pillow front.
- To speed cutting, use a rotary cutter, mat, and ruler.
3. Stitch the strips together (Diagram).

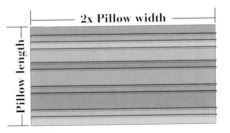

**Diagram**

### Note from Nancy
Gail and I like to add decorative stitching along the right side of each seam line. Set the machine for your favorite decorative stitch, and use rayon or metallic thread and an embroidery or a metallic needle. Place stabilizer on the wrong side of the fabric and stitch. Lovely accents!

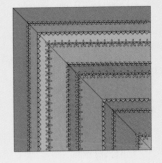

- With right sides together, stitch the strips together along lengthwise edges. Use the edge of the presser foot as a guide for a narrow seam.
- Stitch enough strips together to make patchwork that measures the length of the pillow pattern.
- Press the seams in one direction.
4. Cut out and assemble the pillow front and closure side, following Striped Diagonal Pillows, Step 2.
5. To complete the pillow, follow Step 7 of Basic Pillow, page 52.

# Flange Pillows

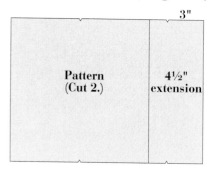

**Diagram A**

2. Cut out the pattern, and mark the fabric with ¼" (6 mm) nips at the marked positions.

3. Add interfacing to the extensions.

• Cut two pieces of fusible interfacing 3" (7.5 cm) wide and the length of the pattern.

• Place interfacing on the wrong side of each pillow rectangle, aligning cut edges as shown. Fuse the interfacing in place (*Diagram B*).

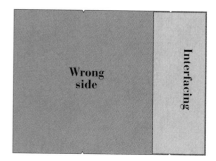

**Diagram B**

*Flanges increase pillow size without requiring a larger pillow form. The flange also serves as a palette for creative accents, such as buttons and blanket stitching.*

## Single-Flange Pillow

### Gather Supplies
Refer to Basic Pillow, page 52, with the following changes:

• ½ yard to ¾ yard (0.50 m to 0.70 m) fabric for 12" to 20" (30.5 cm to 51 cm) square pillow
• Buttons, as desired
• Optional: zipper foot
• Optional: paper-backed fusible web

### Create Single-Flange Pillow
1. Create the pattern.
• Cut a square paper pattern the size of the pillow form plus 1½" (3.8 cm).
• Add a 4½" (11.5 cm) extension to one side to create the flange. (This size extension works for any pillow.)

4. Stitch the pillow sections.
• Use the wrapped-corner technique detailed in Basic Pillow, Step 7, to stitch the side seams and one end seam (*Diagram C*).

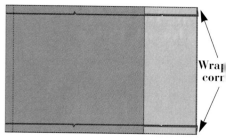

**Diagram C**

- Press seam allowances toward the pillow cover.
5. Fold under a hem on the unsewn edge to create the flange.
- Press the seam open in the flange area. If the fabric is prone to raveling, press under ¼" (6 mm) along the cut edge; stitch (*Diagram D*).

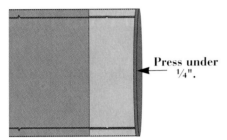

**Press under ¼".**

**Diagram D**

### Note from Nancy

You can finish this edge by fusing. Press a ½"-wide (1.3 cm-wide) strip of paper-backed fusible web to the wrong side of the cut edges. Peel off the paper, fold under ¼" (6 mm), and press.

**Paper-backed fusible web ►**

- Fold the hem under at the 3" (7.5 cm) nip markings; press (*Diagram E*).

**Hem**

**Diagram E**

- Turn the pillow cover right side out.
6. Stitch buttonholes on the flange (*Diagram F*).

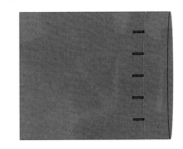

**Diagram F**

- Determine the number of buttons and buttonholes.

- Mark 2" (5 cm) from the hem edge on one side of the flange.
- Mark the buttonholes starting at the 2" (5 cm) line and spacing them an equal distance apart. For ease in positioning, use Space-Tape. (See *Note from Nancy*, page 53.)
- Stitch the buttonholes, sewing through one side of the flange.
7. Handstitch buttons on the opposite side of the flange to correspond to the buttonhole placement. Insert the pillow form.

### Note from Nancy

Buttons and buttonholes make an easy embellishment for a flange pillow. You can choose contrasting, decorative buttons, or make your own using craft clay.

To sew the most professional-looking buttonholes, always sew a test buttonhole first on a fabric scrap. Back the scrap with the interfacing and stabilizer you'll use when sewing the pillow. Be sure to stitch through the same number of fabric layers as the finished pillow will have. If the pillow buttonholes follow the lengthwise grain of your fabric, use that grain for your test buttonhole. If the buttonholes follow the crosswise grain, stitch the test buttonhole along that grain.

For added interest, vary the size and spacing of your buttons and buttonholes, or use mismatched buttons.

# Full-Flange Pillow

## Gather Supplies

Refer to Basic Pillow, page 52, with the following change:

- ½ yard to ¾ yard (0.50 m to 0.70 m) medium-weight fabric for 12" to 20" (30.5 cm to 51 cm) square pillow

## Create Full-Flange Pillow

1. Follow Basic Pillow, Step 1, to create a paper pattern, adding 5½" (14 cm) to the size of the pillow form.
2. Follow Basic Pillow, Steps 2–6, to cut out the pillow sections and to create a pillow back with a closure. Stitch the front and back sections together around the outer edges, wrapping the corners. Turn the pillow cover right side out.
3. Mark and stitch 2" (5 cm) from the outer edge on all four sides (Diagram).
4. Insert the pillow form.

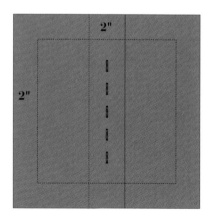

**Diagram**

*Make Full-Flange Pillows (like the blue and tan ones above) from ravel-free fabric, and dress them up with special stitching. The Full-Flange Pillow shown in front is sewn like a basic pillow with an extra row of stitching.*

# Ravel-Free Full-Flange Pillow

## Gather Supplies

Refer to Basic Pillow, page 52, with the following changes:

- ½ yard to ¾ yard (0.50 m to 0.70 m) ravel-free fabric, such as Ultrasuede®, Ultraleather™, or Polarfleece™, for 12" to 20" (30.5 cm to 51 cm) square pillow
- Microtex needle for sewing Ultrasuede
- Optional: 1½ yards to 2½ yards (1.4 m to 2.3 m) trim, cording, or narrow Ultrasuede strips for a weaving finish (blue pillow in photo)
- Optional: Trim, cording, or narrow Ultrasuede strips to measure 4 times the perimeter of the pillow for a blanket-stitch finish (tan pillow in photo)
- Optional: Buttonhole Cutter Set

## Create Ravel-Free Full-Flange Pillow

1. Create and cut out the pattern.
- Cut a square paper pattern the size of the pillow plus 4" (10 cm). Write "Cut 2" on the pattern.
- Cut the pattern out of non-raveling fabric.
- Use a fabric marking pencil to mark 2" (5 cm) from all cut edges on one square *(Diagram A)*.

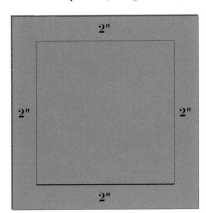

**Diagram A**

### Note from Nancy

Use a Microtex needle for best results stitching Ultrasuede. This needle has a thin shaft and a slim, sharp point that penetrates dense fabric without leaving unsightly holes.

2. Stitch the pillow sections.
- With wrong sides together, stitch along the marked lines on three sides of the pillow.
- Insert the pillow form.
- Stitch the remaining side closed, using a zipper foot (see *Tip from Gail*, page 64).
3. Optional: Add decorative accents to the pillow.

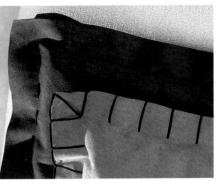

*Woven accents (top) and super-sized blanket stitching finish these Ravel-Free Full-Flange Pillows.*

- **Woven accents:** Mark 1" (2.5 cm) intervals along the stitching line. Place the pillow cover on a wooden cutting block. Use the circular cutter from a Buttonhole Cutter Set to

make cuts just outside the stitching (or use sharp scissors). Make certain the cuts go through both layers. (If desired, you can make these cuts before you stitch the pillow cover together.) Weave trim, cording, or Ultrasuede strips in and out of the holes *(Diagram B)*.

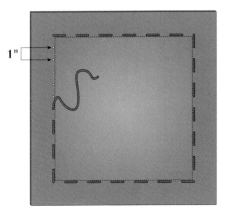

**Diagram B**

- **Super-sized blanket stitching:** Mark at 2" (5 cm) intervals along the stitching line. Use the keyhole blade of a buttonhole cutter or a pair of very sharp scissors to cut holes as indicated for the woven accents. Blanket-stitch the edge using narrow strips of Ultrasuede *(Diagram C)*.

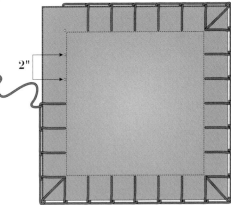

**Diagram C**

*You can add flanges to two sides of a pillow, like the one pictured, to one side only, or to all four sides.*

## Double-Flange Pillow

### Gather Supplies
Refer to Basic Pillow, page 52, with the following changes:
- ⅔ yard to ¾ yard (0.60 m to 0.70 m) fabric for 12" to 20" (30.5 cm to 51 cm) square pillow
- Optional: zipper foot

### Create Double-Flange Pillow
1. Create and cut out the pattern.
- Cut a square paper pattern the size of the pillow form plus 1½" (3.8 cm).
- Add a 4½" (11.5 cm) extension to opposite sides of the square.

- Place nip markings 3" (7.5 cm) from each extension edge at the upper and lower edges. Mark "Cut 2" *(Diagram A)*.

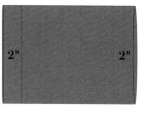

**Diagram A**

- Cut two fabric sections using the pattern.
- Mark the pillow sections with ¼" (6 mm) nips at the marked positions.

2. Add interfacing and sew the pillow as described in Single-Flange Pillow, Steps 3 and 4, page 60, adding flanges at opposite ends. Turn the pillow cover right side out; press.
3. Finish the flange edges.
- Mark 2" (5 cm) from the edge at each end of the pillow.
- Pin along the 2" (5 cm) marked line at one end, making certain the finished edges align.
- Stitch, following the marked line, reinforcing the stitching at both ends *(Diagram B)*.

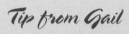

**Diagram B**

- Insert the pillow form.
- Pin along the second marked line, again making certain the finished edges align. Stitch.

### Tip from Gail

Use a zipper foot to ease stitching next to the pillow form. Adjust the needle position to stitch on the line, keeping the pillow form out of the stitching path.

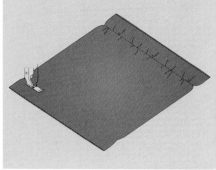

# Envelope Pillows

*Envelope pillows, which are all the rage in home decor magazines, work much like paper envelopes—just tuck the pillow form in the envelope cover and close the flap. Novelty buttons enhance the look and hold the triangular or free-form flap in place.*

## Basic Envelope Pillow

### Gather Supplies
Refer to Basic Pillow, page 52, with the following changes:

- ½ yard to ⅞ yard (0.50 m to 0.80 m) Polarfleece or medium-weight fabric for 12" to 20" (30.5 cm to 51 cm) square pillow
- Optional: Velcro strips
- Optional: button
- Optional: embroidery floss

### Create Basic Envelope Pillow
1. Create and cut out the pattern.
- Cut two square paper patterns the size of the pillow form plus 1½" (3.8 cm).
- Write "Cut 2" on one of the patterns *(Diagram A)*.

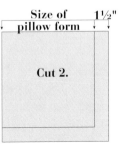

**Diagram A**

- Fold the second pattern in half on the diagonal *(Diagram B)*. Fold it in half again, aligning the folded points. Write "Cut 2" on the pattern *(Diagram C)*.

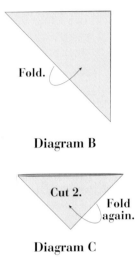

**Diagram B**

**Diagram C**

- Cut out the patterns from the fabric.
2. Stitch the pillow sections.
- Align the pillow squares, right sides together, and pin. Stitch ⅝" (1.5 cm) seams on opposite sides and on one unseamed end, wrapping the seam allowances and cutting the corners at an angle as detailed in Basic Pillow, Step 7.
- Align the envelope flap triangles, right sides together. Pin one of the shorter sides. Stitch, using a ¼" (6 mm) seam allowance *(Diagram D)*.

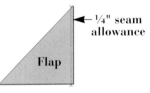

**Diagram D**

*(Continued on page 66)*

- Wrap the seam allowance at the flap point *(Diagram E)*. Pin.

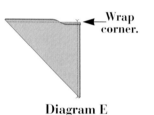

**Diagram E**

- Stitch the second side of the flap, including the wrapped corner. Fold the seam along the stitched seam line. Cut the corner at an angle and press.
- Turn the pillow cover and the flap right side out.
3. Attach the flap to the pillow cover.
- Pin the flap between the seams on one edge of the pillow opening, right sides together.
- Stitch a ⅝" (1.5 cm) seam, sewing around the entire opening *(Diagram F)*. The stitching on the side without the flap provides a pressing guide.

**Diagram F**

- Press under the seam allowance on the side without the flap, following the stitching line *(Diagram G)*.

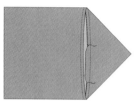

**Diagram G**

- Insert the pillow and handstitch the opening closed.
4. Stitch a buttonhole to the flap and a button on the pillow section.
5. Optional: Add blanket stitching, using embroidery floss.

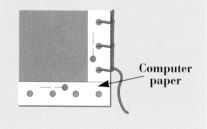
# Free-Form Envelope Pillow

## Gather Supplies
Refer to Basic Pillow, page 52, with the following changes:
- ½ yard to ⅞ yard (0.50 m to 0.80 m) suede, leather, Ultrasuede, Ultraleather, or other leatherlike fabric for 12" to 20" (30.5 cm to 51 cm) square pillow
- 4" (10 cm) length of narrow leather or leatherlike strip or cord
- 1 button

## Create Free-Form Envelope Pillow
1. Create the pattern.
- Cut three paper squares, each the size of the pillow form.
- Tape two patterns together, end to end.
- Fold the third pattern in half on the diagonal. Tape the long side of the triangle to a short end of the two taped patterns. Write "Cut 1" on the pattern.
- Create a leather look on the flap by drawing natural-shaped curves along the short edges of the triangle *(Diagram A)*. If you use real leather, you can simply place the natural curves of the hide edge in the flap area.

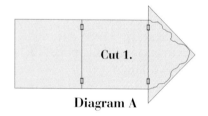

**Cut 1.**

**Diagram A**

3. Cut out the pattern.
4. Stitch the pillow cover.
- Beginning at the end without the flap, fold the square sections with right sides together.
- Stitch the sides, using a ¼" (6 mm) seam *(Diagram B)*.

*Use suede, leather, or look-alikes to make this super-quick envelope pillow.*

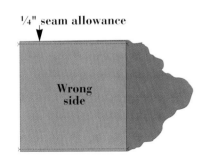

¼" seam allowance

**Wrong side**

**Diagram B**

- Turn the pillow cover right side out. Insert a pillow form.
5. Sew a button to the flap and the leatherlike strip or cord to the pillow, slightly below the flap area. Wrap the tie or the cord around the button.

*Use a border-print fabric or scarf to add flair to a basic envelope pillow.*

# Wrap-up Pillows

*Gathered ties wrap this pillow, creating a soft style. Use drapable fabrics for the ties and their linings. For a variation, consider using a color or texture that contrasts with the basic cover.*

## Fabric Wrap-up

### Gather Supplies
Refer to Basic Pillow, page 52, with the following changes:

- 1¼ yards (1.15 m) lightweight to medium-weight drapable fabric for 12" or 14" (30.5 or 35.5 cm) square pillow
- 2⅞ yards (2.65 m) lightweight to medium-weight drapable fabric for 16" or 18" (40.5 or 46 cm) square pillow
- 4 yards (3.70 m) lightweight to medium-weight drapable fabric for 20" (51 cm) square pillow
- Fashion Ruler™ (for shaping curved edges)

### Create Fabric Wrap-up
1. Create the patterns.
- Cut two square paper patterns the size of the pillow form plus 1½" (3.8 cm). Use one to make the pillow patterns as detailed for Basic Pillow, Step 1.
- Fold the second pattern in half and crease the paper. Fold the paper in half again *(Diagram A)*.

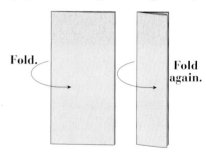

**Fold.**      **Fold again.**

**Diagram A**

- Unfold the paper and repeat, folding and aligning the other two sides. Unfold the paper; the pattern will be gridded into 16 equal squares.
- To create the tie pattern, fold a large sheet of tissue paper in half. Place the gridded pattern on top of the tissue paper, with the tissue paper fold at the top.

# No-Sew
# Self-Tied Bolster

Sophisticated despite its humble creation, this bolster requires no sewing and keeps your fabric intact for effortless recycling. To minimize bulk and maximize draping, select soft fabrics, such as blouse-weight rayons, silky polyesters, and cottons.

## Gather Supplies

2 yards (1.85 m) tightly constructed woven or knit fabric
3 yards (2.75 m) of ½"-wide (1.3 cm-wide) fusible web strips
Bolster form, about 14" long x 6" in diameter (35.5 cm x 15 cm), or 1 roll of 45" x 60" (115 cm x 152.5 cm) quilt batting (See *Tip from Gail* below.)
Optional: 6" (15 cm) length of double-stick carpet tape for securing lapped closure
Optional: flat rubber bands

### Tip from Gail

In my small town of Hoquiam, Washington, where I live, sewing supplies can sometimes be scarce. To create my own bolster forms, I buy inexpensive rolls of quilt batting. The 45" x 60" (115 cm x 152.5 cm) size is sold rolled in perfect bolster dimensions (about 14" long x 6" in diameter or 35.5 cm x 15 cm). I use a long running handstitch to secure the exposed lap. This gives me an instant and inexpensive bolster form that I can reuse later as quilt batting.

## Create No-Sew Self-Tied Bolster

1. Trim the raw edges of the fabric.

### Tip from Gail

To speed sewing and keep your fabric available for recycling, don't trim the fabric width. However, if you use heavier fabric, narrow the fabric width (up to 20" or 51 cm) to reduce bulk.

2. Turn up a 1½"-wide (3.8 cm-wide) double hem on both crosswise edges, and fuse in place *(Diagram A)*. See page 135 for double-hemming tips.

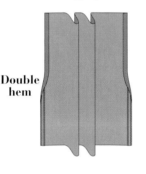

**Double hem**

**Diagram A**

3. Wrap the form with the fabric.
- Fold the fabric in half, lengthwise, wrong sides together.
- Center the bolster form along the selvage edges. About 25" to 30" (63.5 cm to 76 cm) of fabric should extend beyond each end of the form *(Diagram B)*.
- Roll the form toward the fold, keeping the fit snug *(Diagram C)*.
4. Tie the fabric tails *(Diagram D)*.
- Temporarily secure the tails with fat rubber bands.
- Knot each end.
- Clip to remove rubber bands.
5. Optional: Use a 6" (15 cm) strip of carpet tape to close the opening or handstitch closed.

### Tip from Gail

Company coming? Transform your bolsters using large napkins (20" to 26" square or 51 cm to 66 cm square) rather than fabric. Follow Steps 4–6 of "Gathered" Bolster (page 81). You can remove the napkin cover for a decor change or laundering. Now that's "instant interiors!"

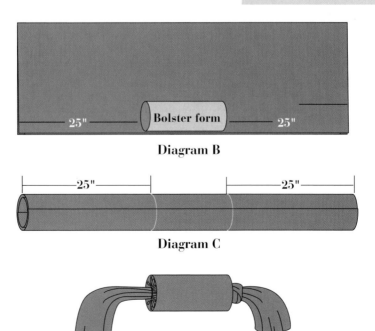

25" — Bolster form — 25"

**Diagram B**

25" — 25"

**Diagram C**

**Diagram D**

*One short session is all you need to complete the ribbon-tied variation (right) of the No-Sew Self-Tied Bolster (left).*

# Ribbon-Tied Bolster

## Gather Supplies

Refer to No-Sew Self-Tied Bolster, page 79, with the following changes:
- Decrease fabric requirement to 1¼ yards (1.15 m)
- 3 yards (2.75 m) grosgrain or satin ribbon, ¼" to 1¼" (2 cm to 3.2 cm) wide (or as desired), or heavy cording

## Create Ribbon-Tied Bolster

1. Follow Steps 1–3 of No-Sew Self-Tied Bolster.
2. Tie the fabric tails.
- Temporarily secure the tails with fat rubber bands.
- Divide the ribbon into two 1½-yard (1.40 m) lengths. Tie the ribbon in a bow around each end of the bolster, over rubber bands *(Diagram)*.

**Diagram**

- If the rubber bands remain exposed, clip to remove them.
3. To close the opening, see No-Sew Self-Tied Bolster, Step 5.

*The gathers of this bolster are controlled with rubber bands—an effective way to make this no-sew pillow look sewn.*

# "Gathered" Bolster

## Gather Supplies

- 27" (68.5 cm) square or ¾ yard (0.70 m) medium-weight, tightly constructed fabric (Heavyweight fabric is also suitable, as long as the gathers don't get too bulky.)
- Bolster form: See No-Sew Self-Tied Bolster, page 79.
- 2 fat (¼"-wide or 6 mm-wide) rubber bands, 5" (12.5 cm) in circumference, such as the type used to bundle letters (Make sure rubber bands are free from news-print ink, which stains fabric.)
- Thread to match
- Optional: 6" (15 cm) length of double-stick carpet tape for securing the lapped closure
- Optional: 2 large tassels or 2 corded "chair tie" tassels

## Create "Gathered" Bolster

1. Use a rotary cutter, mat, and ruler to cut the fabric square accurately.
2. Optional: Finish all edges of the fabric square with pinking, zigzagging, or serging.

---

3. To create the closure hem, fold under 3" (7.5 cm) to the wrong side along one edge and press *(Diagram A)*.

**Diagram A**

4. Cover the bolster.
- Center bolster form along the right side of the hemmed edge *(Diagram B)*.

**Diagram B**

- Roll the form toward the opposite edge, keeping the fit snug. The wrong side of the fabric will show, and the hemmed edge will be concealed.

---

- Secure both ends of the bolster with rubber bands, creating a smooth, taut fit and evenly distributing gathers *(Diagram C)*. Note: If the rubber bands are too tight, they can cut the fabric. Loop them over the gathers just enough to hold. Generally, two to three loops are adequate.

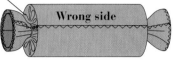

**Diagram C**

- Remove the cover from the bolster and turn it right side out. Reinsert the form with hemmed edge on top *(Diagram D)*.

**Diagram D**

- If necessary, reach inside to arrange the gathers, and pull up on the fabric "ponytail."

5. Optional: Use a 6" (15 cm) strip of carpet tape to close the opening, or handstitch it closed.

6. Optional: Tuck the corded end of a large tassel inside the gathered opening of the bolster end. Repeat for the other end. If necessary, hand-tack to secure.

# Rubber-Banded and Piped Bolster

## Gather Supplies

Refer to "Gathered" Bolster, page 81 with the additions listed below. Fabric requirements and instructions are based on covering a 13"- to 14"-long form with a 6" diameter (33 cm- to 35.5 cm-long with a 15 cm diameter). Yardages vary with form size.

- 1½ yards of ¼"-wide (1.40 m of 6 mm-wide) purchased piping
- Optional: 27" x 13" (68.5 cm x 33 cm) piece of lightweight fusible interfacing, or lining fabric, similar in weight to pillow fabric

## Create Rubber-Banded and Piped Bolster

1. Cut the fabric into rectangles. Vary the dimensions as needed for your pillow.
- Cut one 27" x 13½" (68.5 cm x 34.3 cm) rectangle.
- Cut two 27" x 6" (68.5 cm x 15 cm) rectangles (*Diagram A*).

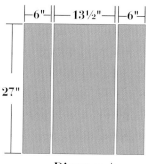

**Diagram A**

2. Optional: Fuse interfacing to, line, or quilt the large fabric rectangle. (See page 129 for interfacing tips.)

For this variation on the "Gathered" Bolster, insert piping to define the edges of the pillow. Unify the design by matching tassel color to the piping.

3. Optional: Finish all fabric edges with pinking, zigzagging, or serging.

4. Check the width of the large rectangle. The finished width (minus seam allowances) should match the bolster width. Narrow as necessary.

5. Insert the piping. (See page 134 for piping tips.)

• Stitch the piping along the right side of the two long edges of the large rectangle, using a ½" (1.3 cm) seam allowance *(Diagram B)*.

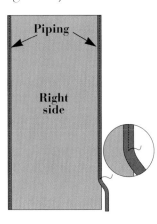

**Diagram B**

• With right sides together, stitch the small rectangles to the large rectangle *(Diagram C)*. Stitch directly over the first stitching line.

**Diagram C**

6. To complete the pillow, follow Steps 3–6 of "Gathered" Bolster.

# Bonus Project: Hybrid Bolster

Gail and I often combine project techniques to fit our time and fabric limitations. We hope to inspire you to experiment, too. The bolster shown here is a good example of a hybrid project: the center section is from Rubber-Banded and Piped Bolster with the ends knotted together like the No-Sew Self-Tied Bolster.

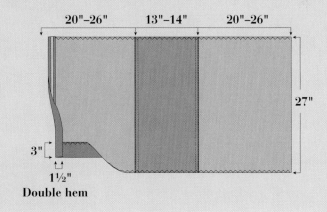

# Dimensional Magic Pillows

*Who would ever have imagined that joining two identical shapes would result in such intriguing three-dimensional pillows? The secret is staggered seaming, created by shifting one of the pieces 90 degrees, rather than the usual matched alignment.*

## TV Room Pillow

When finished, this cushion measures about 22" x 22" x 9" deep (56 cm x 56 cm x 23 cm)—a good size for a TV or study pillow.

### Gather Supplies
- ¾ yard (0.70 m) each of 2 different colors medium-weight, tightly constructed fabric
- Rotary cutter, mat, and ruler
- 3 (12-ounce) bags polyester stuffing
- Thread to match
- Optional: 2½ yards (2.3 m) or 1 package purchased ¼"-wide (6 mm-wide) cotton or rayon piping in contrasting color
- Optional: zipper foot for piping
- Optional: lightweight fusible interfacing

### Create TV Room Pillow
1. Use a rotary cutter, mat, and ruler to cut one 22½" (57.3 cm) square from each fabric color *(Diagram A)*.

**22½"**
**Color 1(Cut 1.)**
**Color 2(Cut 1.)**
**22½"**
**Diagram A**

2. Optional: Fuse interfacing to the pillow squares. See page 129 for interfacing tips.
3. Optional: Apply piping *(Diagram B)*. See page 134 for piping tips.

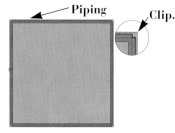

**Piping** — **Clip.**
**Diagram B**

- Stitch piping along the edges of the right side of one square, using a ½" (1.3 cm) seam allowance.
- At the corners, clip into the piping allowances so that the edges lie flat.
4. Seam the cushion.
- Pin the squares right sides together, aligning the corners of one square halfway between the corners of the other square *(Diagram C)*.

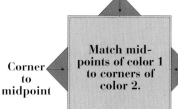

**Corner to midpoint**
**Corner to midpoint** — **Match midpoints of color 1 to corners of color 2.** — **Corner to midpoi**
**Corner to midpoin**
**Diagram C**

- Sew the squares together using a ½" (1.3 cm) seam allowance. If you applied piping, stitch directly over the first stitching line *(Diagram D)*.

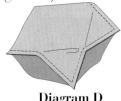

**Diagram D**

- Leave a 6" (15 cm) opening centered between two corners. Turn the pillow cover right side out through the opening.
5. Fill the cushion with small handfuls of polyester stuffing. Fill the corners first (try using the small end of a wooden spoon to position stuffing), then the larger portion.
6. Handstitch the opening closed.

### Tip from Gail

I've discovered that piping helps retain the shape of the corners in these fun pillows. Without piping (especially when using lighter-weight fabrics), these "points of interest" can collapse.

# Bonus Project: Dimensional Ornaments

Miniature Dimensional Magic Pillows make charming tree ornaments, pincushions, and gift tags. Simply follow the instructions, cutting 5" (10 cm) squares or triangles.

# Accent Cube Pillow

## Gather Supplies

- 2 colors medium-weight, tightly woven fabric:
  ⅝ yard (0.60 m) or remnants (each), for small pillow (finished size: about 10" x 10" x 10" or 25.5 cm x 25.5 cm x 25.5 cm)
  1¼ yard (1.15 m) each for medium pillow (finished size: about 20" x 20" x 20" or 51 cm x 51 cm x 51 cm)
- Rotary cutter, mat, and ruler
- 12 ounces polyester stuffing for small pillow or 24 ounces for medium pillow
- ¼"-wide (6 mm-wide) cotton or rayon contrasting-color piping: 1¾ yards (1.60 m) for small pillow or 3½ yards (3.20 m) for medium pillow
- Thread to match
- Optional: zipper foot for piping
- Optional: lightweight fusible interfacing

## Create Accent Cube Pillow

1. Use a rotary cutter, mat, and ruler to cut one equilateral triangle from each color fabric. (Equilateral triangles are the same length on each side.)
- To make the small pillow, cut 21" (53.5 cm) triangles.
- To make the medium-sized pillow, cut 42" (107 cm) triangles (*Diagram A*).

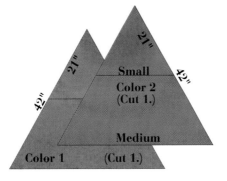

**Diagram A**

2. To complete the pillow, follow TV Room Pillow, Steps 2–4, page 84, substituting "triangle" whenever "square" is specified (*Diagrams B, C, and D*).

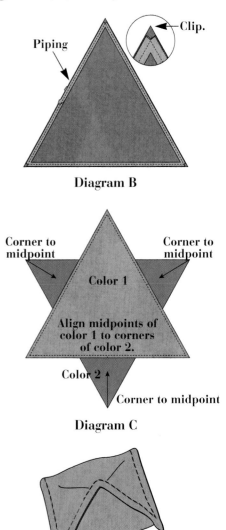

Piping

Clip.

**Diagram B**

Corner to midpoint

Corner to midpoint

Color 1

Align midpoints of color 1 to corners of color 2.

Color 2

Corner to midpoint

**Diagram C**

**Diagram D**

Celebrations

# For the Holidays

*Lining adds body, durability, and easy edge-finishing to a project. But finding a compatible lining fabric can be a challenge. Make shopping and sewing easier by using the project fabric for the lining.*

## Self-Lined Napkins

Inspired by the simplicity of our One-Piece Chevron Pillow (page 74), we applied the same design and construction principles to lined napkins. The construction method creates bias lines, so this napkin is especially lovely when made of fabric with balanced stripes or pronounced textures.

### Gather Supplies

Note: Yardages in this chapter are based on 45"-wide (115 cm-wide) fabric, unless specified otherwise.

- 2 yards (1.85 m) lightweight to medium-weight fabric (makes 4 napkins about 15" or 38 cm square)
- Rotary cutter, mat, and ruler
- Thread to match
- Optional: decorative or contrasting thread for topstitching

# Create Self-Lined Napkins

1. Cut four (22½" or 57.3 cm) squares. For the fastest, most accurate results, use a rotary cutter, mat, and ruler.

## Tip from Gail

Cutting 22½" (57.3 cm) squares makes the most of popular 45"-wide (115 cm-wide) fabric. Because fabric is seldom exactly 45" (115 cm) wide, measure the fabric width first, and divide in half to determine actual square size. If yield isn't crucial, or you're using a wider fabric, cut larger squares to increase finished napkin size. For instance, a 27" (68.5 cm) square yields about a 20" (51 cm) napkin.

2. Seam the napkin.
• Fold the square in half, right sides together, and stitch the ends with a ½" (1.3 cm) seam allowance *(Diagram A)*.

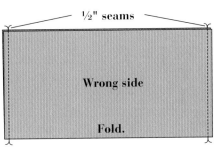

½" seams

Wrong side

Fold.

**Diagram A**

• Press the seams open.
• Clip the seam allowances at the corners.
• Refold, aligning the seam lines.
• Optional: To make sure the napkin will lie flat, press-mark seam allowances *(Diagram B)*. Place the napkin, seam side up, on an ironing board. Narrow or widen the seam to flatten the

napkin, then press. If using a stripe, you can also check matching along the seam line.

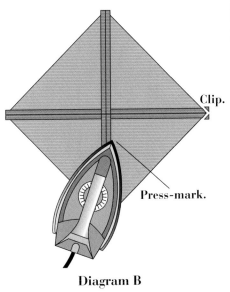

Clip.

Press-mark.

**Diagram B**

• Stitch from each end of the seam, using a ½" (1.3 cm) seam allowance and leaving a 3" (7.5 cm) opening for turning *(Diagram C)*.

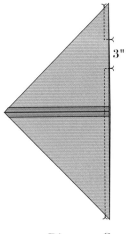

3"

**Diagram C**

3. Turn the napkin right side out.
4. Handstitch the opening closed.
5. From the unseamed side, topstitch the layers together about 1" (2.5 cm) from the edge.
6. Optional: Create decorative topstitching by using a continuous machine embroidery motif.

# Self-Lined Place Mats

A refreshing departure from rectangular place mats, this elegant version dresses up any table for almost any celebration.

## Gather Supplies
• 1 yard (0.95 m) medium-weight fabric (makes 4 place mats about 17" x 20" or 43 cm x 51 cm)
• Thread to match
• Optional: small remnants of lightweight fusible interfacing
• Optional: 1¾ yards (1.60 m) of ½"- to 1½"-wide (1.3 cm- to 3.8 cm-wide) flat trim, such as ribbon
• Optional: 1 button per place mat, ½" to 1" (1.3 cm to 2.5 cm) in diameter, to secure tassel
• Optional: 1 tassel per place mat, about 3" (7.5 cm) long, or as desired

*(Continued on page 90)*

## Create Self-Lined Place Mats

1. From the fabric, cut a rectangle 36" wide x 21" long (91.5 cm wide x 53.5 cm long).
2. Seam the place mat *(Diagram A)*.

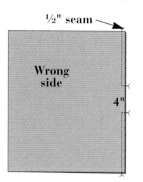

**Diagram A**

- With right sides together, fold the rectangle in half lengthwise.
- Stitch a ½" (1.3 cm) seam, centering a 4" (10 cm) opening.
- Refold the rectangle, centering the seam lengthwise. Press the seam open.
3. Stitch the ends.
- Fold the corner points to the center as shown *(Diagram B)*, overlapping the center seam line about ½" (1.3 cm). The point will be about ¼" to ½" (6 mm to 1.3 cm) from the raw edges.

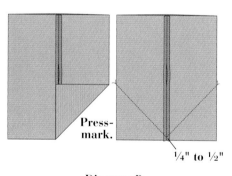

**Diagram B**

- Press-mark the folds.
- Stitch along the press markings, being careful not to stretch the bias edge (the V-shaped stitching lines) as you sew.

- Trim seam allowances to about 1" (2.5 cm) wide, narrowing at the point.
- Stitch a ½" (1.3 cm) seam at the other end of the place mat.
4. Turn right side out through the opening in the center back seam. Press.
5. Handstitch the opening closed, or fuse the edges with a ¾" x 5" (2 cm x 12.5 cm) piece of lightweight fusible interfacing. (See page 129 for interfacing tips.)
6. Optional: Decorate the place mat edges in one of the following ways:
- Topstitch *(Diagram C)*.

**Diagram C**

- Sew flat trim to the place mat ½" to 1" (1.3 cm to 2.5 cm) from the finished edges.
7. Optional: Sew a button to the point end, centering it on the topstitching or ribbon, or ½" to 1" (1.3 cm to 2.5 cm) from the point. Hang a tassel on the button. Remove tassel when you clean the place mat *(Diagram D)*.

**Diagram D**

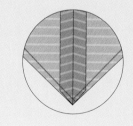
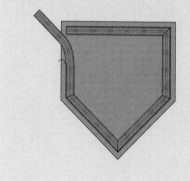

## Create Self-Lined Runner

1. Cut out the runner from fabric.
- For a 44"-long (112 cm-long) runner, cut a rectangle 36" x 45" (91.5 cm x 115 cm).
- For a longer runner or for one that is longer than the fabric width, cut two rectangles, each 36" (91.5 cm) wide by half the desired finished length plus 1" (2.5 cm).

2. If necessary, piece the runner. Stitch two short ends of the rectangles, right sides together, using a ½" (1.3 cm) seam allowance.

3. Follow Steps 2–6 of Self-Lined Place Mats to complete the runner. Embellish the runner as desired. If you pieced the runner, cover the seam with ribbon or trim first, and then embellish the edges *(Diagram)*.

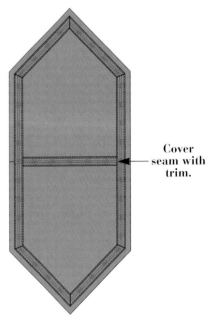

Cover seam with trim.

**Diagram**

*This stylish runner can double as place mats. Just arrange the length across the table width, from setting to setting.*

## Self-Lined Runner

### Gather Supplies

- 1 yard (0.95 m) of fabric makes 1 runner 17" x 44" (43 cm x 112 cm); 2 yards (1.85 m) makes 1 runner 17" wide x up to 88" long (43 cm wide x 223.5 cm long). Runner is cut on crosswise grain and pieced at center. For lengthwise-grain runner with no center seam, yardage required is finished length plus 1" (2.5 cm).
- Thread to match
- Optional: Small remnants lightweight fusible interfacing
- Optional: 3 yards (2.75 m) ½"- to 1½"-wide (1.3 cm- to 2.8 cm-wide) flat trim for 44" (112 cm) runner, or 6 yards (5.5 m) for 88" (223.5 cm) runner.
- Optional: 2 buttons
- Optional: 2 tassels

*Mantel scarves are making a big comeback on the decorating scene, both for holidays and for everyday decorating. These versatile accessories even look great accenting pianos, sideboards, and dressers. If this scarf looks familiar, you're right: it's made from Self-Lined Place Mats (page 89), pieced together and bordered.*

# Mantel Scarf

## Gather Supplies

- 1 yard (0.95 m) medium-weight fabric or 3 place mats for 1 (68" x 20" or 173 cm x 51 cm) scarf
  2 yards (1.85 m) medium-weight fabric or 4 place mats for 1 (85" x 20" or 216 cm x 51 cm) scarf

Measure your mantel to decide how many place mats to make.

- Thread to match
- 1½ yards (1.40 m) of ¾"- to 1½"-wide (2 cm- to 3.8 cm-wide) ribbon for small scarf or 2 yards (1.85 m) ribbon for large scarf
- Optional: remnant lightweight fusible interfacing

- Optional: for ribbon-trimmed scarf, increase trim yardage to 5 yards (4.60 m) for small scarf or 6 yards (5.5 m) for large scarf
- Optional: 3 or 4 tassels
- Optional: 3 or 4 buttons
- Optional: 3 or 4 small brass bells (in place of tassels and buttons)
- Optional: monofilament thread

# Create Mantel Scarf

1. Make three place mats (four for a large scarf), following Steps 1–5 of Self-Lined Place Mats, page 90.

2. For the scarf end pieces, cut two 12" (30.5 cm) squares from place mat fabric.

3. Create end pieces (Diagram A).

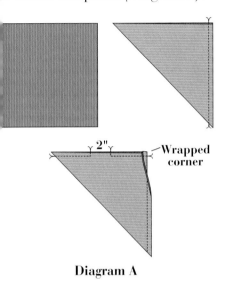

**Diagram A**

- Fold each end piece in half diagonally, right sides together, forming a triangle.
- Stitch each end piece using ½" (1.3 cm) seam allowances and wrapping corners. Leave a 2" (5 cm) opening for turning.
- Turn each end piece right side out and press.

4. Optional: Edgestitch ribbon to the pointed ends of the place mats and to the folded edges of the end pieces (Diagram B). For easiest folded mitering, see page 90.

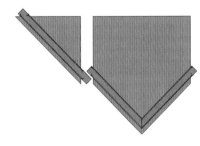

**Diagram B**

- Wrap raw edges of the ribbon to the underside of the place mat.
- When applying ribbon, use a short ruler to ensure that the ribbon is the same distance from all edges.

5. Optional: If you prefer a more traditional scarf look (that's also quicker to make), topstitch the place mat edges, and finish the corners with buttoned-on tassels (see page 90).

6. Assemble the scarf (Diagram C).

- Cut wide ribbon into four (or five) 13" (33 cm) lengths.
- Center ribbon pieces (or edge-finished fabric) wherever place mat edges and end pieces meet. Pin in place.
- Turn under the ribbon ends to align with finished scarf edges.
- From the right side, topstitch through all layers, joining the place mats to each other and to the end pieces.

7. Optional: Handstitch bells to the points of the scarf.

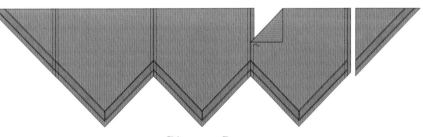

**Diagram C**

## Tip from Gail

My tall fireplace needed a finished look on the exposed underside of the scarf, so I devised a reversible ribbon scheme (see photo below). This uses ¾ yard (0.70 m) more ribbon per place mat but application is easy. Using monofilament thread, edgestitch ribbon to the underside of the pointed edges. Wrap ribbon to the front; edgestitch again. (With opaque ribbon, fuse it to the underside first.) To avoid mitering translucent ribbon and gain textural layering, crisscross ribbon at corners.

## Tip from Gail

Decorate for the holidays with a festive—and easy—napkin fold. (Use our Self-Lined Napkins, page 88.) Create a dazzling table setting by placing these "trees" over each plate or on a buffet.

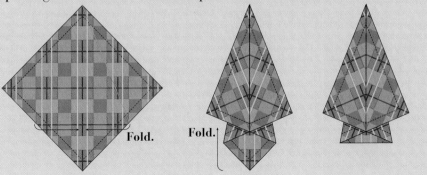

*Adapt this centerpiece to fit the season, or use it as a gift for any occasion. The design is simple, incorporating a napkin and other basic shapes that are a cinch to sew or serve. Wiring maintains the handle curve.*

# Fabric Basket Centerpiece

## Gather Supplies

- 45"-wide (115 cm-wide) medium-weight cotton fabric
  ⅓ yard (0.30 m) each 2 coordinating fabrics, or 2 (12" or 30.5 cm) square napkins for base
  ⅛ yard (0.15 m) of a third coordinating fabric for handle
- ½ yard 45"-wide (0.50 m 115 cm-wide) crisp, decorator-weight fusible interfacing
- ⅛ yard 45"-wide (0.15 m 115 cm-wide) paper-backed fusible web
- Thread to match
- 5 yards to 7½ yards (4.60 m to 6.90 m) #20-gauge wire
- Paper or craft scissors
- Ribbon or other trim
- Optional: fabric marker

## Create Fabric Basket Centerpiece

1. Cut out the fabric pieces.
- For the base, cut two 12" (30.5 cm) squares from the coordinating cotton fabrics, or use two 12" (30.5 cm) napkins.
- Cut two 12" (30.5 cm) squares from fusible interfacing for the base.
- For the handle, cut one 4" x 45" (10 cm x 115 cm) strip each from handle fabric, fusible interfacing, and fusible web.
2. Join the base fabric squares.
- Fuse interfacing to the wrong sides of both fabric squares or napkins.
- With right sides together, stitch around the edges, wrapping the corners (see Basic Pillow, page 52) and leaving an opening for turning. Turn right side out and close the opening with hand-stitching or fusible web.
- Or with wrong sides together, serge the edges together. (See

pages 132–133 for serge-finishing options.)
3. Create the handle.
- Fuse the interfacing to the wrong side of the handle fabric.
- Press the paper-backed fusible web to the interfacing.
- Mark the lengthwise center of the handle with pins or a marker. With wrong sides together, fold the long edges to meet at the center marking. Finger-press in place, creating a 2"-wide (5 cm-wide) strip *(Diagram A)*.

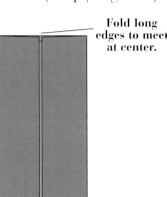

Fold long edges to meet at center.

**Diagram A**

- Cut several 45" (115 cm) lengths of wire. Twist two or three strands together. Repeat, creating two 45"-long (115 cm long) twisted strands.
- Unfold the handle; remove the paper backing from the web. Position the wires on the wrong side of the handle, near the pressed creases at each edge. Fold the fabric over the wires; press, fusing the layers and encasing the wires *(Diagram B)*.

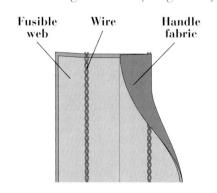

Fusible web          Wire          Handle fabric

**Diagram B**

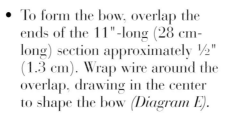
• Cut the handle into one 26"-long (66 cm-long) piece and one 19"-long (48.5 cm-long) piece, using paper or craft scissors.

4. Stitch the handle to the fabric base.

• Cut the 19"-long (48.5 cm-long) section into two 4"-long (10 cm-long) pieces and one 11"-long (28 cm-long) piece.

• To form the tails, fold one end of each 4"-long (10 cm-long) section, right sides together, aligning the edges. Stitch a ¼" (6 mm) seam across the end and turn the tails right sides out *(Diagram C)*.

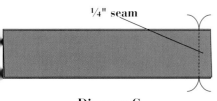

**Diagram C**

• Position the tails on the right side of the base square at one corner as shown. Hand- or machine-tack *(Diagram D)*.

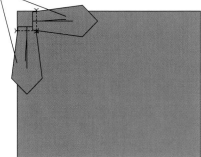

**Diagram D**

• To form the bow, overlap the ends of the 11"-long (28 cm-long) section approximately ½" (1.3 cm). Wrap wire around the overlap, drawing in the center to shape the bow *(Diagram E)*.

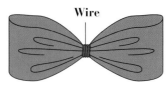

**Diagram E**

• Working from the wrong side, measure 3" (7.5 cm) from one end of the 26"-long (66 cm-long) section. Form a loop by bringing the cut end to the measured point. Secure with handstitching or machine bartacking *(Diagram F)*.

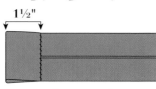

**Diagram F**

• Tuck the bow under the loop.

• Position the handle diagonally across the fabric square or napkin, with the bow at one corner and the handle extending past the opposite corner. Zigzag the handle to the base, stitching next to the wire *(Diagram G)*.

**Diagram G**

• Tuck the unstitched end of the handle under the bow. Handstitch the bow in place, covering the end of the handle.

5. Embellish the basket with ribbon or other trim.

# Bonus Project: Holiday Centerpiece

Create a larger holiday version of the Fabric Basket Centerpiece by increasing the napkin size to 15" (38 cm). For the handle, fuse motifs from preprinted yardage. Rather than make a fabric bow, form a coordinating accent from 2 yards (1.85 m) of purchased wire-edged ribbon.

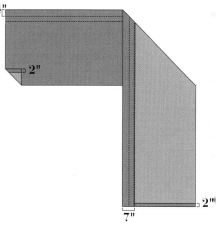

**Diagram A**

- From the right side, stitch 7" (18 cm) from the fold. Backstitch at both ends.
4. Mark the hem *(Diagram B)*.

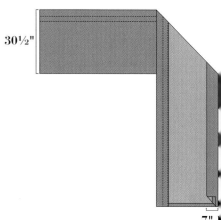

**Diagram B**

- Fold under 7" (18 cm), adjusting hem depth to yield a 30½"-deep (77.3 cm-deep) skirt.
- Pin and press.
5. Embellish the casing and hemline edges *(Diagram C)*.

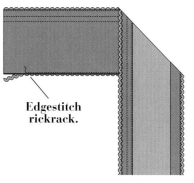

Edgestitch rickrack.

**Diagram C**

*You'll love this tree skirt. The look is luxurious, but it's sewn flat—and fast. Much like a drawstring dirndl skirt, it adjusts to fit most Christmas tree trunks, and the soft gathers visually balance even the most heavily decorated tree.*

# Gather-to-Fit Tree Skirt

## Gather Supplies
- 5¼ yards (4.80 m) medium-weight fabric for skirt
- Thread to match
- 10 yards (9.15 m) jumbo rickrack
- 1½ yards (1.40 m) soft lamé, chiffon, or lining fabric for ties
- Optional: 5 yards (4.60 m) of ¼"-wide (6 mm-wide) or wider piping or cording
- Optional: monofilament thread

## Create Gather-to-Fit Tree Skirt
1. Finish the crosswise edges of the skirt fabric. (See pages 33–35 for edge-finishing options.)
2. Fold under 2" (5 cm) at each crosswise end of the fabric and press. Stitch in place ½" (1.3 cm) from the pressed edge.
3. Stitch the casing *(Diagram A)*.
- Fold under 7½" (19.3 cm) and press.
- From the right side, stitch 4" (10 cm) from the fold. Backstitch at both ends.

- Lap the casing over jumbo rickrack so that the rickrack's scallops peek out from the edge; pin. Repeat for hem.
- Edgestitch the rickrack in place, lapping where necessary to piece the trim.
6. Tuck and stitch the hemline edge *(Diagram D)*.

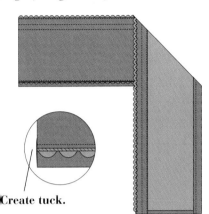

**Create tuck.**

**Diagram D**

- Optional: Trim the hemline edge with piping or cording, sandwiching piping/cording between the hemline fold and the rickrack. (See page 134 for piping tips.) The piping's seam allowance will be hidden by the tuck, which you form next.
- Fold to form a 1½" (3.8 cm) tuck along the hemline edge. The depth of the skirt with the tuck should be 32".

# Bonus Project: No-Sew Tree Skirt

In a hurry? Create an instant "skirt" by simply draping three or more yards of fabric under your tree. Gail and I each confess to relying on this no-sew solution!

—Nancy

- Edgestitch, stitching directly over the piping/cording and rickrack stitching lines.
- From the right side, stitch about 4½" (11.5 cm) from the hemline fold, or 1" (2.5 cm) less than the hem depth. Backstitch at both ends.
7. Create the soft tie *(Diagram E)*.
- Cut the tie fabric into 18"-wide (46 cm-wide) strips.
- Piece as necessary to make a 3-yard (2.75-m) fabric strip.
- With right sides together, fold the strip in half lengthwise.
- Stitch a ½" (1.3 cm) seam along the long edges, centering a 4" (10 cm) opening for turning.
- Center the seam and then use a rubber band to gather the edges at each end of the tie.
- Turn the tie right side out through the opening. Do not press.
- Use a bodkin or a large safety pin to thread the tie through the casing.

- Pull to gather the skirt and tie in a soft bow.

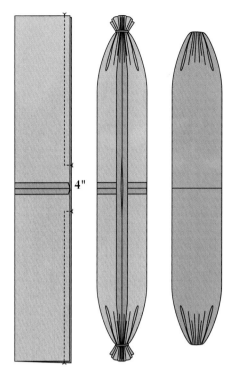

4"

**Diagram E**

*This tree skirt's dramatic tie is so simple to make! The tie ends are softly gathered in an instant with household rubber bands.*

# For Him

*Does a "Remote Man" reign in your life? Join the club! Organize his television-watching world by making a caddy for the television schedule and his precious channel changer.*

## Armchair TV Caddy

### Gather Supplies
- ½ yard (0.50 m) medium-weight to heavyweight fabric, such as denim, canvas, or tapestry
- Rotary cutter, mat, and ruler
- Thread to match
- Optional: contrasting thread for topstitching
- Optional: Radial Rule

### Note from Nancy

A Radial Rule is a notion used to round corners quickly and accurately. Align the straight edges of the rule with the border or edges of your project, and cut using a rotary cutter.

### Create Armchair TV Caddy
1. Cut the base, backing, and pockets.
- Cut two 24" x 9" (61 cm x 23 cm) rectangles of the fabric for the base and the backing.
- Cut three 12" x 9" (30.5 cm x 23 cm) rectangles of the fabric for the pockets.
2. Set one pocket piece aside. Round all four corners on the remaining pieces, using a saucer or a Radial Rule to cut curves *(Diagram A)*.

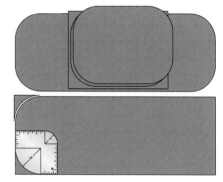

**Diagram A**

3. Place the pockets on the base fabric.
- Fold each pocket section in half, wrong sides together, aligning the short ends.
- Optional: Using contrasting color thread, edgestitch the pockets, and then stitch again ¼" (6 mm) from the folded edge.
- Clean-finish the squared pocket raw edges by zigzagging or serging them together.
- Position the squared pocket so that the clean-finished edges are 5" (12.5 cm) from one end; pin or baste in place. Stitch the bottom edge of the pocket in place along the clean-finished edge *(Diagram B)*.

**Diagram B**

# Bonus Project: Armchair Sewing Caddy

You can easily adapt Armchair TV Caddy instructions to create an Armchair Sewing Caddy. Follow Steps 1 and 2, cutting the backing fabric 5" (12.5 cm) shorter than the base fabric and cutting only two pocket sections. Follow Steps 1 and 2. Then fold the base in half, wrong sides together, aligning short ends. Stitch 2½" (6.3 cm) from the fold *(Diagram AA)*. Stuff the stitched section with batting to create a pincushion. Flatten the ends of the section; center the seam, and machine-baste each end closed *(Diagram BB)*. Follow Steps 3–5, adding two pockets, rather than three, in Step 3.

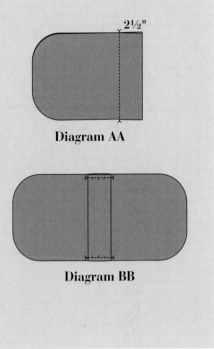

**Diagram AA**

**Diagram BB**

---

- Position the remaining pockets at each end of the base section, matching the curves. Pin or baste in place *(Diagram C)*.

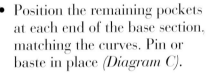

**Diagram C**

4. Line the caddy.
- With right sides facing, place backing section and base section together.

- Stitch or serge the outer edges using a ½" (1.3 cm) seam, and leaving a 5" (12.5 cm) opening *(Diagram D)*. Trim the seam.

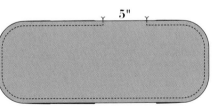

5"

**Diagram D**

- Turn the caddy right side out and stitch the opening closed.
- Optional: Edgestitch as in Step 3.

5. Topstitch pockets as desired to create dividers *(Diagram E)*.

**Topstitch to create divider.**

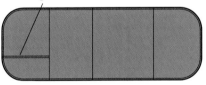

**Diagram E**

## Create Stuffed-Shirt Pillow

1. Optional: Add shoulders to the pillow form (*Diagram A*).

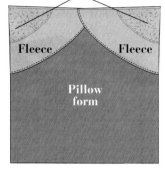

**Diagram A**

- Hand-baste the shoulder pads to the pillow form.
- Cover the pads with one to two layers of polyester fleece or batting. Hand-tack to the pillow form cover. (See *Tip from Gail* on page 101.)

2. Fit the shirt to the pillow form (*Diagram B*).

*Poke some good-natured fun at your favorite "stuffed shirt." Buy an inexpensive shirt or retire one of his over-worn wearables, and transform it into his special pillow. Consider giving the pillow and the Stuffed-Shirt Laundry Bag (page 102) as a set.*

**Diagram B**

- Unbutton or unsnap the shirt.
- Turn the shirt inside out.
- Center the pillow form inside the shirt and refasten the front placket.
- Pin to fit the shirt to the pillow form.
- Cut off excess fabric, leaving about 1" (2.5 cm) seam allowances (*Diagram C*). Save excess fabric and sleeves. Remove the pillow form.

## Stuffed-Shirt Pillow

### Gather Supplies

- 1 (20" or 51 cm) square or larger pillow form, or purchased or recycled pillow
- 1 men's shirt, any size, although small and medium shirts fit purchased pillow forms better. Textured or heavy woven fabrics and colorful plaids work well.
- Thread to match
- Optional: 1 bandanna or handkerchief in contrasting color (you use only half)
- Optional: 1 pair large shoulder pads (to add "shoulders" to pillow form)
- Optional: scraps of polyester fleece or bonded batting (to cover shoulder pads and fill out pillow form)
- Optional: few ounces polyester stuffing (to fill out pillow corners)

**Diagram C**

3. Seam the shirt to create the pillow cover.
- Using the pin markings as a guide, baste the side and lower edge seams, right sides together.
- Try the shirt on the pillow form again to fine-tune the fit. Remember if it's too loose, the shirt can look sloppy.
- Trim the seam allowances to about ½" (1.3 cm).
- Restitch the side and lower edge seams, wrapping the corners.
- Turn the shirt right side out.

4. Insert the pillow form through the front shirt opening.

5. Fill out corners and neckline with extra stuffing and fleece.

6. Cover the exposed pillow form at the neckline *(Diagram D).*

**Diagram D**

- Cut a 5" (12.5 cm) square from leftover sleeve or hem fabric. (If the shirt pockets are bias, consider cutting the square on the bias, also.)
- Position the square inside the neckline opening, to cover the pillow form.
- Hand-tack in place, hiding the stitches under the shirt collar.

7. Optional: Put a bandanna in the left front shirt pocket *(Diagram E).*

**Bandanna half**

**Diagram E**

- Cut the bandanna in half, to minimize bulk. (You can use the other half for the Stuffed-Shirt Laundry Bag, page 102.)
- Hand-tack to secure.

8. Optional: Hand-tack the placket and neckline opening to the form. Hide the stitches under the placket tuck and in the seam indentation of the collar stand.

*Tip from Gail*

After Step 1, I hold the shirt up to the pillow form and ask, "How will the pockets look when the pillow is covered?" I find that if I skip this step the pockets are too low on the pillow (probably because my husband is an XL-sized guy). To correct this problem, I extend the length of the pillow by rolling up fleece or batting and tacking it to the lower edge of the pillow form. Buffer the surface, if necessary, by covering it with one more piece of fleece, hand-tacking it in place. The shirt covers any bumps in your altered pillow form.

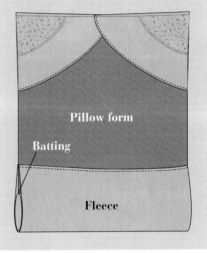

Pillow form

Batting

Fleece

- Unbutton or unsnap the shirt.
- Turn the shirt inside out.
- Place the hanger inside the shirt and refasten the front placket.
- Pin to fit the side seams to the hanger width. The fit should be slightly loose around the hanger, not too tight.
- Trim off excess fabric, leaving 1" (2.5 cm) seam allowances.

3. Seam the shirt to create the laundry bag.
- Using the pin markings as a guide, baste the side seams, right sides together.
- Trim the seam allowances to about ½" (1.3 cm), and finish the edges. (See pages 33–35 for edge-finishing options).
- Turn the shirt right side out.

4. Topstitch the lower edges of the shirt, wrong sides together *(Diagram C)*. You may need to pleat the center back at the hem. If so, copy the pleat at the yoke.

*Banish boring laundry bags! Rescue an overused, underused, or fashionably dysfunctional shirt, and in one short sewing session, renew it as a fun, practical laundry bag.*

# Stuffed-Shirt Laundry Bag

## Gather Supplies
- 1 men's shirt, any size; larger sizes (L, XL, and XXL) accommodate more laundry. Durable, tightly woven shirts, such as denim, work well.
- Clothes hanger
- Thread to match
- Optional: 1 pair large shoulder pads (for adding shape to hanger)
- Optional: 1 bandanna or hankie in contrasting color (only half is used)

## Create Stuffed-Shirt Laundry Bag

1. Optional: Hand-baste shoulder pads to the hanger *(Diagram A)*.

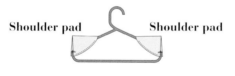

**Shoulder pad**        **Shoulder pad**

**Diagram A**

2. Fit shirt to hanger *(Diagram B)*.

**Diagram B**

**Topstitch.**

**Diagram C**

5. Follow Step 7 of Stuffed-Shirt Pillow (page 101) to finish the laundry bag.

# For New Arrivals

*Anyone who's proud of a new arrival deserves bragging rights. And what better way to open the accolades than with a photo wallet? Sew one that's uniquely yours (or theirs), and show off darling babies of any age.*

## Photo Wallet

### Gather Supplies

- ¼ yard (0.25 m) heavyweight fabric, such as canvas or denim
- 2 (8½" x 11" or 21.8 cm x 28 cm) sheets clear vinyl, or 2 transparent report covers
- Sewing machine needle, size 90 or 100
- Thread to match
- 1¾ yard (1.6 m) or 1 package ¼"-wide (6 mm-wide) double-fold bias tape
- 1 button, ½" (1.3 cm) diameter
- Optional: Radial Rule (see *Note from Nancy*, page 98)

### Create Photo Wallet

1. Cut the fabric.
- Cut a 5½" x 24" (14 cm x 61 cm) piece of heavyweight fabric.
- Cut five 3¾" x 5½" (9.5 cm x 14 cm) rectangles of vinyl.
2. Assemble the wallet.
- Round off the corners of the heavyweight fabric using a Radial Rule or a saucer *(Diagram A).*

**Diagram A**

- Lay the vinyl pieces horizontally along the fabric, beginning 2" (5 cm) from one end and leaving ¼" (6 mm) between each vinyl piece.
- Insert a size 90 or 100 needle in your sewing machine. Create five pockets by edgestitching the vinyl to the fabric along one side and along the top and bottom edges *(Diagram B).*

**Diagram B**

- Form a 1½" (3.8 cm) loop from bias tape. On the outside of the wallet, center the loop at the bottom and baste *(Diagram C).*

**Diagram C**

- Starting at the end opposite the loop, fold the bias tape along the raw edges and edgestitch, covering the stitched sides of the pockets. Where the tape ends meet, turn the end under ¼" (6 mm) and stitch in place. (See page 130 for bias binding tips.)
- Starting at the end without the loop, fold into a wallet shape, covering the vinyl windows.
- On the outside center a button on the end opposite the loop. Hand-sew in place.

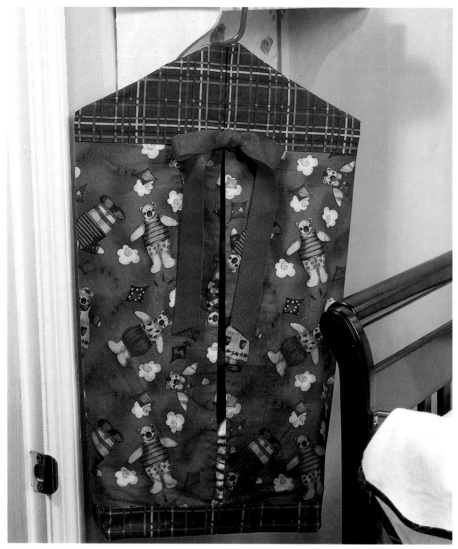

*Make this multipurpose hamper in minutes, as a gift or for your own home. You can hang it in a baby's room as a diaper stacker, in the bathroom for towel storage, or in a bedroom as a laundry bag.*

# Hanging Hamper

## Gather Supplies
- 1⅛ yards (1.05 m) medium-weight fabric in main color
- ½ yard (0.50 m) medium-weight fabric in accent color
- ¼ yard (0.25 m) lightweight to medium-weight fusible interfacing
- Thread to match
- Fabric marker
- 2½ yards (2.30 m) 1½"- to 2"-wide (3.8 cm- to 5 cm-wide) grosgrain or other stable, durable ribbon
- 1 large safety pin
- 4¼" x 13¼" (10.5 cm x 33.5 cm) piece foam-core board or heavy cardboard
- 1 full-size, sturdy plastic or upholstered hanger to coordinate with fabric colors
- Optional: Staple gun and staples (Swing-open desktop models are adequate.)
- Optional: 1 yard (0.95 m) 1"- to 3"-wide (2.5 cm- to 7.5 cm-wide) adhesive tape
- Optional: monofilament thread

## Create Hanging Hamper
1. Cut out the hamper *(Diagram A)*. Following the cutting guidelines below yields a finished length of 28" (71 cm). Adjust the main fabric length as desired to vary the finished length. Cut all pieces the full fabric width (about 45" or 115 cm).

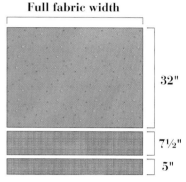

**Diagram A**

- From the main fabric, cut a 32" (81.5 cm) length.
- From the accent fabric, cut one 7½" (19.3 cm) length (for the upper end) and one 5" (12.5 cm) length (for the lower end).
- Cut the interfacing 5" by 45" (12.5 cm by 115 cm).

2. Fuse interfacing to the wrong side of the 5" (12.5 cm) piece of accent fabric.

3. Position and sew the accent fabric pieces to the main fabric *(Diagram B)*.

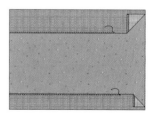

**Diagram B**

- Press under ½" (1.3 cm) on one long edge of each accent piece.
- Pin the wrong sides of the accent pieces to the right side of the main fabric, aligning raw edges.
- Edgestitch the accent pieces to the main fabric.

4. Shape the hamper to the hanger *(Diagram C)*.

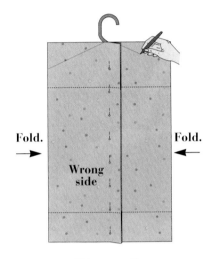

**Diagram C**

- Fold the fabric right side over the hanger, centering the fabric edges at the center of the hanger. Pin to mark the opening. The fit should be slightly loose.
- Using a fabric marker, trace the top of the hanger on the wrong side of the fabric.
- Fold a 2" to 3" (5 cm to 7.5 cm) double hem on each side of the opening and stitch in place. (Adjust hem width to fit your fabric width and hanger size.) Press and topstitch, using your presser foot as a guide. (See page 135 for double hem tips.)
- Center the double hems on the fabric, right sides together.

- Stitch along the markings, leaving a centered 1" (2.5 cm) opening for inserting the hanger. Trim the seam allowances to ½" (1.3 cm) *(Diagram D)*.

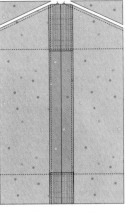

**Diagram D**

5. Shape the lower edge of the hamper.
- Stitch a ½" (1.3 cm) seam *(Diagram E)*. Finger-press the seam open.

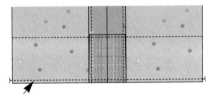

½" seam

**Diagram E**

- Box the corners by refolding as shown in *(Diagram F)*.

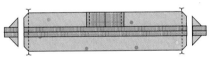

**Diagram F**

- Center and stitch a 4"-long (10 cm-long) seam. Trim to ½" (1.3 cm) and finish the edges (see pages 33–35). Repeat for the other corner.

6. Create the windowed seam for the opening *(Diagram G)*.

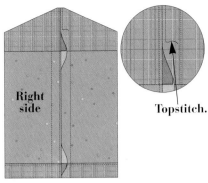

Right side

Topstitch.

**Diagram G**

- Cut ribbon into one 7" (18 cm) length and one 5½" (14 cm) length.
- Center the longer ribbon at the top opening, under the accent fabric. Fold any excess ribbon to the wrong side. Pin.
- Center the shorter ribbon at the lower opening, under the accent fabric. Fold any excess ribbon to the wrong side. Pin.
- Topstitch through all opening layers on both sides, using your presser foot as a guideline.

7. Tie a bow with leftover ribbon. Using a large safety pin, fasten bow to hamper above the opening.

8. Optional: Cover the board with fabric *(Diagram H)*.

**Diagram H**

- Cut a 6" x 15" (15 cm x 38 cm) piece of the main fabric.
- Center the board on the wrong side of the fabric.
- Working side to side, wrap fabric around the board and staple in place.
- Optional: Finish raw fabric edges with adhesive tape.

9. Place the foam-core board or cardboard in the hamper, finished side up.

10. Insert the hanger. Hang hamper on a doorknob, closet rod, or wall hook. (Remove bow and board before laundering hamper).

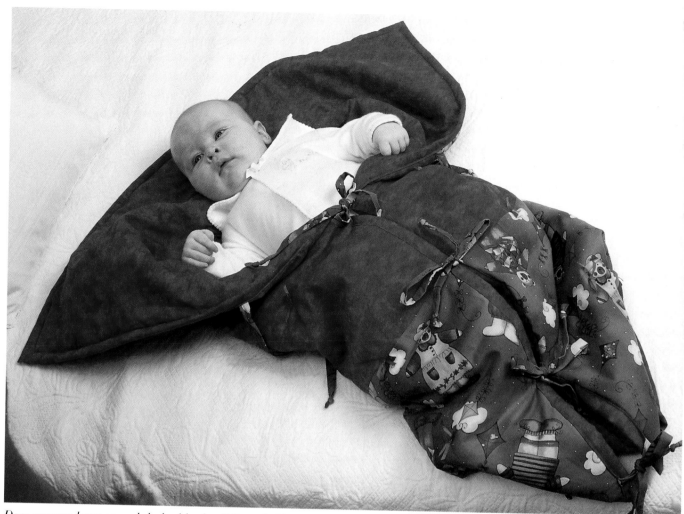

*Does anyone have enough baby blankets? Remedy blanket shortages—and please parents on your gift list—by quickly sewing or serging this versatile baby blanket. Tied, this bunting becomes a snuggly. Untied, it lies conveniently flat to serve as a napping or changing mat.*

# Tied Baby Bunting

## Gather Supplies

- Lightweight to medium-weight cotton or flannel:
  Color A: 1⅞ yards (1.75 m)
  Color B: ⅞ yard (0.80 m)
- Rotary cutter, mat, and ruler
- Thread to match
- 1 yard (0.95 m) 45"-wide (115 cm-wide) low-loft (8-ounce polyester) batting
- Curved basting pins
- 3 yards (2.75 m) embroidery floss or silk ribbon
- Optional: Fasturn® tube turner
- Optional: 5 yards (4.60 m) 1"-wide (2.5 cm-wide) ribbon (to use instead of fabric for ties)

## Create Tied Baby Bunting

Note: All seam allowances are ¼" (6 mm).

1. Cut the fabric using a rotary cutter, mat, and ruler.

- From Color A, cut four 11" x 14" (28 cm x 35.5 cm) rectangles for the top, and one 1-yard (0.95-m) length for backing.
- From Color B, cut five 11" x 14" (28 cm x 35.5 cm) rectangles for the top, and five strips for the ties (*Diagram A*).

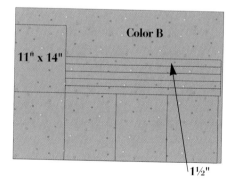

**Diagram A**

2. Prepare bunting top *(Diagram B)*. To make Rows 1 and 3, with right sides together and long sides aligned, stitch three rectangles in the following order: Color B, Color A, Color B. Press seams toward Color B.
Stitch Row 2 the same way as Rows 1 and 3, but in the following order: Color A, Color B, Color A. Press seams toward Color B. Stitch the three rows to each other, right sides together and matching the seams. Press the seams toward the bottom.

|  | Color B | Color A | Color B |
|---|---|---|---|
| Row 1 | | | |
| Row 2 | A | B | A |
| Row 3 | B | A | B |

**Diagram B**

3. Prepare the ties.
- With right sides facing and long edges aligned, stitch the tie strips. Turn, strips with a Fasturn. (See page 135.) Cut the ties into 11" (28 cm) lengths, or cut ribbon into 12" (30.5 cm) lengths.
- Baste ties to the bunting top *(Diagram C)*. Knot the free ends of the ties.

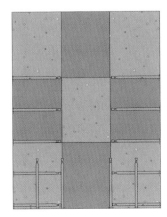

**Diagram C**

4. Assemble the bunting.
- Cut the batting to fit the bunting top.
- Stack the backing, batting, and top as follows: backing, wrong side up; batting; and top, right side up.
- Trim the backing, leaving a 1¼" (3.2 cm) margin on each side of the top/batting layers.
- Baste or pin the layers together with curved basting pins, starting in the center and working toward the edges.
- Using embroidery floss or silk ribbon, tie the basted layers together at the rectangle intersections, midpoint seam lines, and centers *(Diagram D)*.

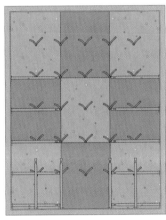

**Diagram D**

Optional: machine-bartack as a substitute for hand-tying.
5. Bind the bunting.
- Fold the corner of the backing up over the corner of the bunting front, forming a triangle. Trim the triangle to reduce bulk *(Diagram E)*.

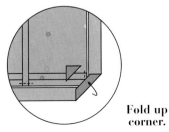

Fold up corner.

**Diagram E**

- Fold the backing so that its edges align with the edges of the bunting top *(Diagram F)*.

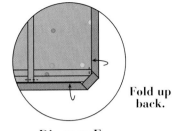

Fold up back.

**Diagram F**

- Fold the backing once more at the edge of the bunting top to create the binding, mitering the corners. Pin in place *(Diagram G)*.

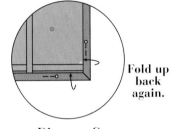

Fold up back again.

**Diagram G**

- Stitch the binding in place by hand or by machine.
6. For comfort and warmth, place the baby on the solid side of the bunting, fold the long edges to the middle and tie the lower ties.

*Note from Nancy*

To save time and fabric, substitute 1"-wide (2.5 cm-wide) washable ribbon for the tie strips. Or if you want to make a quick flat quilt, eliminate the ties altogether.

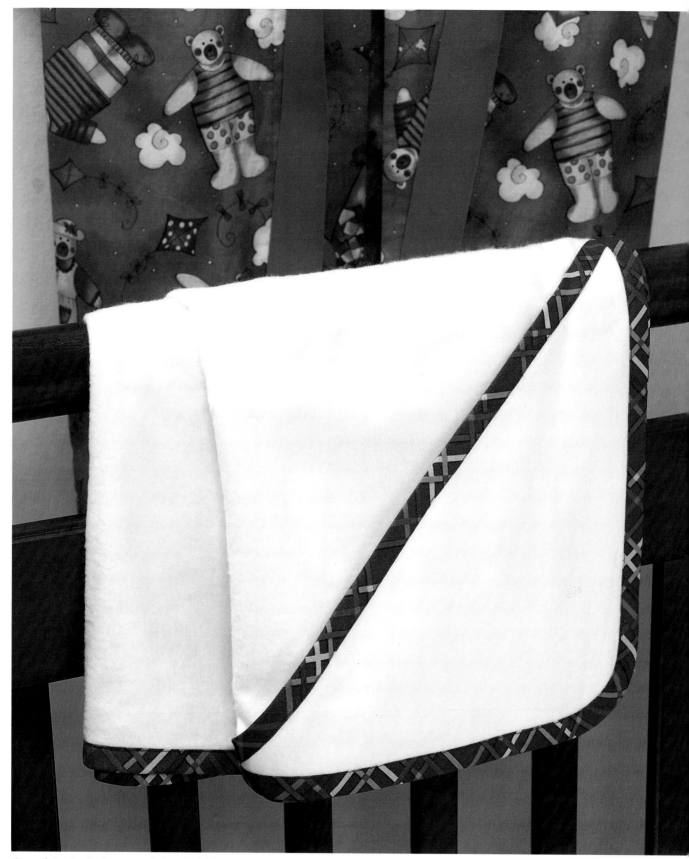

*Out of the bath, into a soft, hooded blanket—your baby (or a baby on your gift list) will delight in the instant warmth and comfort of this custom wrap.*

# Bath Towel Blanket

## Gather Supplies

1¼ yards (1.15 m) flannel or terry cloth

4½ yards (4.15 m) extra-wide double-fold bias tape

Thread to match

Optional: Radial Rule (see *Note from Nancy*, page 98)

## Create Bath Towel Blanket

1. Cut the fabric.
   Cut a 35" (89 cm) square for the blanket.
   Cut a 12" (30.5 cm) square of paper and fold it in half diagonally. Use the triangle shape to cut out the hood.

2. Assemble the bath towel blanket *(Diagram)*.

**Diagram**

- Round off the square's corners and the point of the hood, using a saucer, plate, or Radial Rule.
- Bind the diagonal edge of the hood with bias tape. (See page 130 for bias binding tips.)
- Place the wrong side of the hood on the right side of one blanket corner, aligning the raw edges. Baste the hood in place.
- Bind the edges of the blanket with bias tape. To finish the binding, turn the end under ¼" (6 mm) and overlap the starting point of the bias tape before stitching.

# Bonus Project: Receiving Blankets

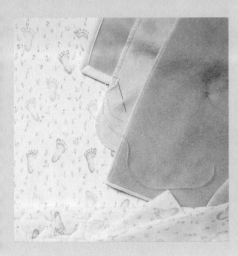

Use coordinating colors and prints of flannel or Polarfleece to make several extra-large receiving blankets. Simply cut the fabric into 35" (89 cm) squares, rounding the corners if desired. Finish the edges with one of the following options:

- Stretch binding—see page 34 for how to use Seams Great to finish edges.
- Blanket stitching—see page 66 for how to blanket-stitch edges.
- Serging—see page 132 for how to serge-finish edges.

*Finish receiving blankets with your choice of edging: (from left) stretch binding, blanket stitching, and serging.*

# Speedy Pillowcases

*Pillowcases are high on our list of favorite projects. Incredibly easy to sew, they double as palettes for decorative trim, ruffles, or machine stitches. Your personalized pillowcases will get raves—plus orders for more!*

## Basic Pillowcase

### Gather Supplies
- 1⅛ yard to 1⅜ yard (1.05 m to 1.30 m) medium-weight cotton
- Thread to match

### Create Basic Pillowcase
1. Cut the fabric into a rectangle to fit your pillow.
- **Standard:** 38" x 41" (96.5 cm x 104 cm)
- **Queen:** 42" x 41" (107 cm x 104 cm)
- **King:** 48" x 41" (122 cm x 104 cm)

2. Fold the rectangle in half, right sides together, aligning the 38" (96.5 cm) edges. (Align 42" or 107 cm edges for a queen-size and 48" or 122 cm edges for a king-size pillowcase.) Stitch or serge across one end, using a ½" (1.3 cm) seam. Wrap the corner by folding the seam toward the pillowcase along the stitching line and stitch or serge the side seam *(Diagram A)*.

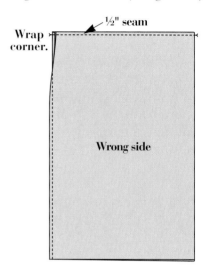

**Diagram A**

3. To make a double hem on the open end of the pillowcase, fold and press a 4" (10 cm) hem. Fold again at 4" (10 cm), press, and topstitch the hem in place.

## Trimmed Pillowcase

### Gather Supplies
Refer to Basic Pillowcase with the following addition:
- 2" (5 cm) crosswise strip of contrasting fabric for trim

### Create Trimmed Pillowcase
1. Cut the pillowcase fabric into a rectangle to fit your pillow.
- **Standard:** 28" x 41" (71 cm x 104 cm)
- **Queen:** 32" x 41" (81.5 cm x 104 cm)
- **King:** 48" x 41" (96.5 cm x 104 cm)

2. From the pillowcase fabric, cut a 9" x 41" (23 cm x 104 cm) rectangle for the hem.
3. Fold the trim in half, wrong sides together, aligning the lengthwise edges; press. Pin the trim to the right side of the large rectangle, aligning raw edges with one long edge *(Diagram B)*. Baste in place.

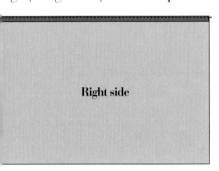

**Diagram B**

4. Fold the large rectangle in half, right sides together, aligning the short ends. Stitch or serge, following Step 2 of Basic Pillowcase.
5. With right sides together, stitch or serge the ends of the 9" x 41" (23 cm x 104 cm) rectangle. Fold

and press, wrong sides together, aligning the lengthwise edges. Pin over the trim, and stitch or serge the layers together. Clean-finish raw edges if not serged.

## Ruffled Pillowcase

### Gather Supplies
- 1⅜ yards to 1⅝ yards (1.30 m to 1.50 m) 45"-wide (115 cm-wide) medium-weight cotton fabric for pillowcase and ruffle
- 2" (5 cm) crosswise strip 45"-wide (115 cm-wide) contrasting cotton fabric for trim
- Thread to match

### Create Ruffled Pillowcase
1. Cut the fabric.
- Cut a rectangle from the pillowcase fabric, following Step 1 of Trimmed Pillowcase.
- Cut two 9" (23 cm) crosswise strips of fabric for the ruffle.
2. Follow Steps 3 and 4 of Trimmed Pillowcase.

3. Stitch the short ends of the ruffle fabric, right sides together. Fold and press, wrong sides together, aligning the lengthwise edges. Gather the raw edges to fit the pillowcase opening. (See page 131 for gathering techniques.)
4. With right sides together, stitch or serge the ruffle to the pillowcase and trim. Clean-finish raw edges if not serged. Topstitch the trim along the ruffled edge *(Diagram C)*.

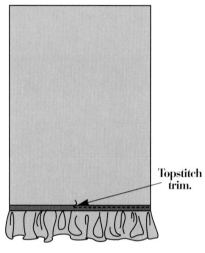

Topstitch trim.

**Diagram C**

# Bonus Project: Monogrammed Pillowcases

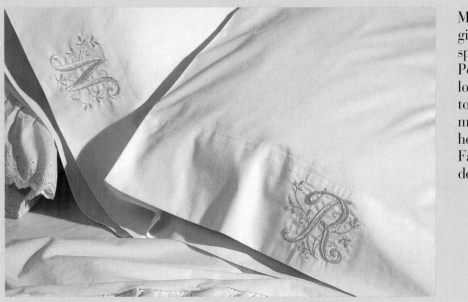

Make a quick yet elegant gift for a bridal shower or a special treat for yourself. Personalize a pair of pillowcases using a tone-on-tone, machine-embroidered monogram on the pillowcase hem. I used Pfaff's Creative Fantasy Card #16 for this design.

## Quickest

## Quicker

## Quick

# *Furoshiki* Fabric Wrap

*Furoshiki is a Japanese term for fabric squares used to wrap gifts or to carry shopping items. Gail and I call them "gifts wrapping gifts," because these elegant squares double as hankies, napkins, scarves, totes, table toppers, and pillow covers.*

The idea makes sense for anyone who sews—simply use fabrics from your stash as gift wrap. No paper can rival the color, texture, or negligible cost of your quick-to-make fabric creations. Best yet, these environment-friendly gift wraps can be used again and again. Or the recipient can turn them into charming fashion or home decor accessories.

## Unlined Fabric Wrap

### Gather Supplies
Yardages given in this chapter are based on 45"-wide (115 cm-wide) fabric unless noted otherwise.

- Lightweight to medium-weight fabric
  **Small wrap:** ⅝ yard (0.60 m) makes two 20" (51 cm) squares
  **Medium wrap:** 1 yard (0.95 m) makes one 36" (91.5 cm) square
  **Large wrap:** 1¼ yards (1.15 m) makes one 45" (115 cm) square
  **Blooming wrap:** 1 yard (9.95 m) makes one 36" (91.5 cm) circle
- For fused edges: 2¼ yards to 5 yards (2.10 m to 4.60 m) of ¾"-wide (2 cm-wide) fusible web
- For serged edges: All-purpose thread or serger thread to match

### Create Unlined Fabric Wrap

1. Referring to dimensions under Gather Supplies, cut the fabric into a square for a small, medium, or large wrap, or cut a circle for a blooming wrap. To cut a circle, fold the fabric in half lengthwise; then fold it in half crosswise. Using a pushpin, string, and a pencil to make a compass, mark a circle *(Diagram A)*. Cut through all layers along marked lines.

**Diagram A**

2. Finish edges of the square using one of the following options.
- Fuse the edge *(Diagram B)*. Working from the wrong side, press fusible web strips to the edges of two opposite sides of the square. Remove the paper backing; fold the edges to align with the inner edge of the fusible web; press. Repeat for remaining sides. Optional: Pink edges before removing fusible web strips.

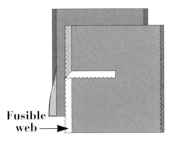

**Diagram B**

- Serge a rolled edge (see page 132).

3. Wrap your gift using one of the options shown in the diagrams on this page and page 116. If you don't have enough fabric to tie or knot the corners, fasten the wrap with a fat rubber band. (For fabric gift tags and embellishments, see instructions beginning on page 123.)

## Simple Wrap

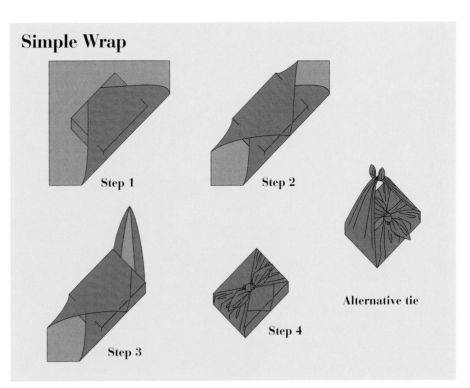

Step 1

Step 2

Step 3

Step 4

Alternative tie

## Bottle Wrap

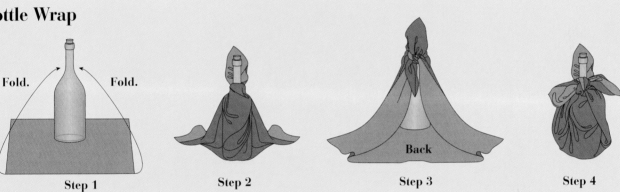

Step 1

Step 2

Step 3   Back

Step 4

## Double Bottle Wrap

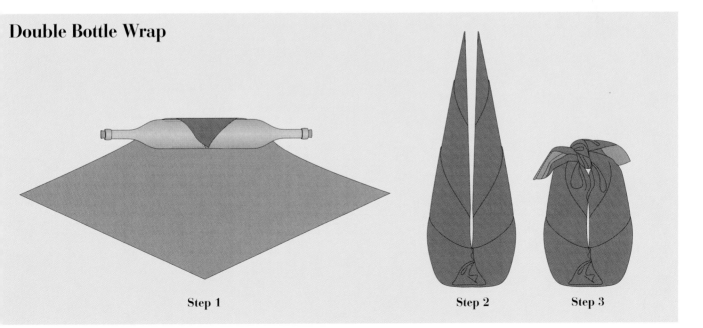

Step 1

Step 2

Step 3

## Blooming Wrap

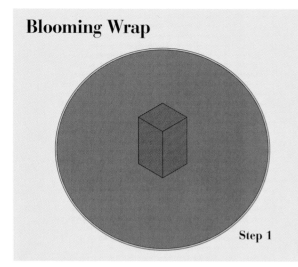

Step 1

Step 2

**Blooming Wrap on small box**

## Bouquet Wrap

Step 1

Step 2

Step 3

# Bonus Project: Serged-Edge *Furoshiki* Wrap

If you finish your *furoshiki* wrap with narrow rolled edges, you can make the serging easier by cutting the wrap into a circle (the same diameter as the desired square), or by rounding the corners of square wraps. Then serge over 25- to 30-gauge beading wire or 20- to 25-pound fishing line. The filler adds a malleable curl to the edges, allowing you to shape the wrap.

For a variation, serge a 13" (33 cm) circle using fishing line or wire. When knotted, this size makes a lovely bow. If you use fishing line, this wrap can double as a Blooming Hanky (see Bonus Project, page 35). Wired edges, unless very lightweight, can be too stiff for fashions, so reserve them for decor projects.

- Press the seam allowances flat; then fold the seams toward the center along the stitching lines and press. Pin the corners. This wraps the seam allowances, making it easier to get sharp corners.
- Stitch the remaining side seams, leaving an opening for turning. Cut the corners at an angle *(Diagram B)*.

**Diagram B**

*Tip from Gail*
To serge-finish lined wraps, place squares wrong sides together and finish with a narrow rolled-edge or narrow unrolled edge. (See pages 132–133.)

If hairy edges are a problem, try this terrific tip: Fuse the edges together first, using ½"-wide (1.3 cm-wide) fusible web strips. The web stabilizes the fibers, ensuring ravel-free serged edges.

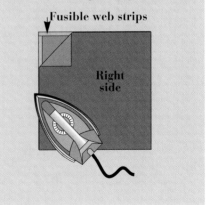

*A contrasting lining adds flair to these* Furoshiki *wraps.*

# Lined Fabric Wrap

## Gather Supplies
Note: for contrasting linings, buy half as much fabric in each of 2 colors.

- Lightweight to medium-weight fabric
  **Small wrap:** ⅝ yard (0.60 m) makes one 20" (51 cm) square
  **Medium wrap:** 2 yards (1.85 m) makes one 36" (91.5 cm) square
  **Large wrap:** 2½ yards (2.30 m) makes one 45" (115 cm) square
  **Blooming wrap:** 2 yards (1.85 m) makes one 36" (91.5 cm) circle
- All-purpose thread or serger thread to match

## Create Lined Fabric Wrap
1. Referring to Gather Supplies for measurements, cut two squares or circles of fabric for each wrap.
2. With right sides together, stitch the squares or circles, using ¼" (6 mm) seams.
- For a circle: stitch a continuous seam, leaving an opening for turning.
- For a square: stitch two opposite sides *(Diagram A)*.

**Diagram A**

3. Wrap your gift using one of the options in Unlined Fabric Wrap, Step 3.

# Gift Sacks

*Surprisingly versatile, Lined Gift Sacks wrap a wide range of box, jar, and bottle sizes. Those lucky enough to receive them will discover myriad uses for them, such as jewelry cases, travel organizers, and shoe bags.*

## Lined Gift Sack

### Gather Supplies

- Lightweight to medium-weight taffeta, brocade, satin, lamé, cotton, or flannel:
  **To wrap wine bottle, quart jar, bread, or long or medium box:** ½ yard (0.50 m) each of 2 contrasting fabrics makes 2 sacks; ½ yard (0.50 m) of 1 fabric makes 1 self-lined sack.
  **To wrap pint/jelly jar or small box:** ¼ yard (0.25 m) each of 2 contrasting fabrics makes 3 sacks; ½ yard (0.50 m) of 1 fabric makes 3 self-lined sacks.
- Thread to match

### Create Lined Gift Sack

1. Cut the fabric according to dimensions below. We've suggested sizes, but you can cut any dimensions that best use your remnants or fit your gifts.
- **Wine bottle, quart jar, or long box:** Cut two 14" x 18" (35.5 cm x 46 cm) rectangles.
- **Bread or medium box:** Measure bread (or the cylinder from your bread-making machine) or measure box. Add 2" to the circumference and 7" to the length; cut two rectangles this size.
- **Pint/jelly jar or small box:** Cut two 8" x 12" (20.5 cm x 30.5 cm) rectangles.

2. Stitch lining, using ¼" (6 mm) seams and leaving a 2" (5 cm) opening for turning *(Diagram A)*.

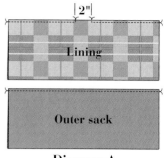

**Diagram A**

- **Wine bottle, long box, bread, or medium box:** With right sides together, stitch the long sides.
  **Quart jar, pint/jelly jar, or small box:** With right sides together, stitch the short sides.
- Fold the lining (wrong side out) with the seam centered. Stitch the lower edge *(Diagram B)*.
- Refold the lining, centering the bottom-edge seam; finger-press the seam open. Stitch across the corners of the bag, beginning and ending 1" (2.5 cm) from the points *(Diagram C)*. Trim the corners.

     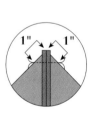

**Diagram B**          **Diagram C**

3. Repeat Step 2 to stitch the outer sack, without an opening for turning.
4. Assemble the sack.
- Turn the outer sack right side out and slip it inside the lining sack, right sides together. Pin top edges together.
- Stitch the top. Turn the sack right side out through the liner

opening, and stitch the opening closed.

- Fold the sack along the top edge, tucking the lining inside the outer sack.
5. Fold and tie the sack in one of the following ways (shown in the photo on page 110 from left to right):
- Embellish and close the sack with a Tack-a-Bloom. For directions, see page 123.
- Cuff the top edge, turning the lining to the right side. To shorten the sack for smaller items, fold the top edge over twice.
- Use a ribbon to close the opening, arranging the top to expose the lining.

*Turn linings on Lined Bottle Sacks for an easy finished look.*

- Close the top with rubber bands. Hide the bands under the cuff or under a ribbon tie. Rubber bands work especially well with jars; you can leave the metal lids uncovered and the rubber bands hold the cuff snug to the rim.
- Simply tie a ribbon around the opening.

*For easy Unlined Gift Sacks, make them from Polarfleece and embellish them with (left to right) jelly rolls, appliqué, two-tone design, or contrasting serged edge.*

## Unlined Gift Sack

### Gather Supplies
- ¼ yard to ½ yard (0.25 m to 0.50 m) of ravel-free fleece, such as Polarfleece; synthetic suede; or chamois cloth
- Thread to match
- Optional: Pinking shears or rotary cutter with pinking or wave blade
- Optional for fusible fleece accents:
  Fusible web remnants (or 1 small package of fusible web)
  Fabric glue or adhesive
  Small sew-on metal bells or buttons

### Create Unlined Gift Sack
1. Make the sack following Lined Gift Sack directions on page 118, eliminating the lining. Keep in mind that unlined knit and fleece fabrics stretch to fit a wide range of package, bottle, or jar sizes.
2. Leave the sack top unfinished, or finish it one of the following ways:
- Use pinking shears or decorative rotary-cutting blades.
- Zigzag or machine-stitch the edges with a decorative stitch.
- Serge the edges with a narrow rolled-edge stitch or create lettuce edges (see pages 132–133).
3. Embellish the sack in one of the following ways:
- Appliqué a tree (or a design of your choice) on the sack before stitching the seam. Cut triangles in three graduated sizes using the pattern on page 142. Stitch each triangle (working from largest to smallest) ⅛" (3 mm) from the edge. Overlap the triangle points by 1" (2.5 cm) as you build the tree. Embellish as desired with bells or buttons as ornaments *(photo above)*.
- Fringe the top edge of the sack. Cut slits about 2" to 3" (5 cm to 7.5 cm) deep and ⅜" (1 cm) apart *(photo below)*.

- Use two contrasting colors of fleece to create a two-tone sack (see photo, far right). Optional: Zigzag sack seamlines, top, and tie strip edges.
- Weave a ribbon or a narrow strip of Ultrasuede through slits cut 2" (5 cm) apart and starting 2" (5 cm) below the upper edge of the sack. Tie the ribbons or strips into a bow. Optional: Cut two rows of slits, ½" to 1" (1.3 cm to 2.5 cm) apart, alternating the slit spacing.
- Have fun with reversible fused fleece. Using fusible web, fuse the wrong sides of two pieces of contrasting-color fleece. Use this double-sided fabric to make unique tie accents:

# Bonus Project: Elegant Sacks

For that special birthday, shower, or wedding, use chiffon or other sheer fabrics to create an elegant gift sack. Serge the seams with a rolled-edge stitch. To close the sack, tie with ribbon, or simply tie this soft, lightweight fabric into a knot or a bow. Accent with a purchased or serged-chain tassel (see page 133).

## Jelly Roll

•• For jelly rolls *(photo above):* Rotary-cut the double-sided fabric into a ⅜"-wide (1 cm-wide) strip about 11" (28 cm) long *(Diagram A)*. Put fabric glue on the strip and roll it into a jelly roll *(Diagram B)*. Cut a ⅜"-wide (1 cm-wide) strip about 10" to 15" (25.5 cm to 38 cm) long, and handstitch the jelly roll to one end of this strip *(Diagram C)*. Optional: Sew a small bell to the jelly roll.

**11"**

⅜"

**Diagram A**

**Diagram B**          **Diagram C**

## Fat Tassel

•• For fat tassels *(photo above):* Rotary-cut the double-sided fabric into a 4" x 5" (10 cm x 12.5 cm) rectangle. Fringe one long edge *(Diagram D)*. Roll up the rectangle, gluing to secure *(Diagram E)*. Hand-stitch a reversible strip to the center of the rolled end, sewing on a small bell, if desired *(Diagram F)*.

**Diagram D**

**Diagram E**          **Diagram F**

•• Tie tips: To strengthen fused-fleece ties, edgestitch with straight stitching or zigzagging. To shorten ties, simply wrap them around the sack two or more times.

# Gift Wrap Gifts

*Need to wrap an oddly shaped present or a lot of small gifts? This jumbo stocking sack is roomy enough to hold your wrapping challenges beautifully and safely.*

## Super-Sized Stocking Sack

### Gather Supplies

- 1 yard (0.95 m) each of light-weight to medium-weight fabric in a main color and a contrasting lining color
- Thread to match
- Tissue paper
- Optional: Contrasting all-purpose or embroidery thread (for decorative stitching)
- Optional: 2½ yards (2.30 m) of ¼"-wide (6 mm-wide) satin cord for monogramming

### Create Super-Sized Stocking Sack

1. Using the pattern on page 136, enlarge the pattern 250% on a photocopy machine. The finished stocking is about 25" x 19" (63.5 cm x 48.3 cm), so you'll have to copy it in pieces. Or copy the toe section and extend the top to equal approximately 25" (63.5 cm).

2. Cut two stocking pieces each from the main and the contrasting lining fabrics.

3. With right sides together, pin and stitch the sides, using a ¼" (6 mm) seam allowance.

4. Repeat Step 3 to stitch the lining pieces together, leaving a 3" (7.5 cm) opening in one side seam for turning.

5. Clip the seam allowances in the curved areas. Press the seams flat and then press them open.

6. Turn one stocking right side out and slip it inside the other stocking, right sides together. Pin and stitch along the top.

7. Turn the stocking right side out through the opening in the lining. Stitch the opening closed. Fold the stocking along the top, tucking lining inside outer stocking. Fold down the top 2" to 4" (5 cm to 10 cm), creating a cuff and exposing the lining.

8. Optional: To make a loop, cut a 14" (35.5 cm) strip of ¾"- to 1"-wide (2 cm- to 2.5 cm-wide) ribbon or fabric. Zigzag the ends together to form a loop *(Diagram)*. Center inside the cuff seam, so that a 3½"-long (9 cm-long) loop extends beyond the cuff section fold. From the right side, stitch-in-the-ditch to secure.

9. Optional: Topstitch along the cuff edge using a decorative stitch.

10. Optional: To monogram the cuff, use a wide, medium-length zigzag with ¼" (6 mm) satin cord. Mark the name on the cuff with a temporary fabric marker, place the cord over the drawn letters, and zigzag the cord in place.

11. Place gifts inside the stocking.

12. Optional: To keep gifts away from curious eyes, close stocking top with machine- or hand-basting, hiding the stitches under the cuff.

**Diagram**

*Everyone—even your friends and relatives who don't sew—must deal with mending emergencies, such as popped buttons, ripped seams, and hanging hems. Our Mending Sack can rescue him or her, providing the requisite buttons, pins, needles, and threads, all gathered together in a gift-worthy tote.*

# Mending Sack

## Gather Supplies

- ¼ yard (0.25 m) each of solid-color and contrasting light-weight to medium-weight cotton fabric
- 12" (30.5 cm) of ribbon or decorative cording
- Thread to match
- Buttons in styles and colors suitable for shirts, blouses, trousers, and jackets
- Travel sewing kit, or hand-sewing needles, small scissors, and thread
- Optional: needle threader, small tape measure, thimble, and other small sewing notions

## Create Mending Sack

1. Cut the fabric.
- For the sack, cut one 5" x 12" (12.5 cm x 30.5 cm) rectangle from solid-color fabric and one from contrasting fabric.
- For the pocket, cut one 5" x 8" (12.5 cm x 20.5 cm) rectangle from contrasting fabric.
- Use the pattern on page 136 to cut one heart shape from contrasting fabric for the appliqué.
- With wrong sides together, align the short edges of the solid-color fabric. Press to create a fold line.

2. Appliqué the heart to the solid-color rectangle, referring to *Diagram* for placement. (See page 128 for tips on appliquéing.)

3. With right sides together, align and stitch the short edges of the pocket. Turn right side out and press. Place the seamed edge of the pocket along the fold line of the sack and edgestitch.

4. Place each end of the ribbon or cording about ⅜" (1 cm) below the top corners of the sack and baste within the seam allowances.

5. With right sides together, align the short ends of the solid-color rectangle; pin and stitch the sides. Repeat for the contrasting rectangle (lining), leaving a 3" (7.5 cm) opening in one seam for turning.

6. Turn one sack right side out and slip it inside the other sack, right sides together. Pin and stitch along the top.

7. Turn the sack right side out through the opening in the lining and stitch the opening closed. Fold the sack along the top, tucking the lining inside the outer sack.

8. Embellish as desired with handstitched buttons on the heart.

9. Place a travel sewing kit, or hand-sewing needles, small scissors, and other sewing notions in the pockets.

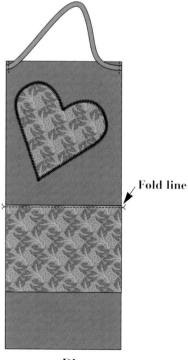

**Fold line**

**Diagram**

# Embellishments

Dress up fabric gift wraps with a Tack-a-Bloom (left and center packages) or a tassel (right).

## Tack-a-Bloom

This floral accent may look complex, but it's really quite simple. A flat strip of fabric "blooms" when you pull ribbon drawstrings through strategically placed bar tacks. The Tack-a-Bloom looks great on packages and makes a colorful accent for your hair, a hat, or a lapel.

### Gather Supplies
- ⅛ yd (0.15 m) of lightweight to medium-weight taffeta, brocade, satin, or cotton
- 2 yards (1.85 m) of ⅛"-wide (3 mm-wide) ribbon
- Thread to match

### Create Tack-a-Bloom
1. Cut a 4½" x 36" (11.5 cm x 91.5 cm) strip of fabric. Angle-cut the ends (Diagram A). Serge or clean-finish the ends. (See page 135 for clean-finishing techniques.)
2. Attach ribbon to the fabric strip.

**Diagram A**

- With wrong sides together, fold the fabric strip in half, aligning short ends. Pin the lengthwise edges together.
- Cut the ribbon into two 1-yard (0.95-m) lengths. Fold each length in half.
- Center each ribbon fold at the fold of the fabric strip. Stitch

the ribbons to the fabric fold (Diagram B).
3. Stitch or serge the lengthwise edges of the strip with ¼" (6 mm) seams, being careful not to catch the ribbons in the seam. If using a conventional sewing machine, clean-finish the exposed edges.
4. Turn the strip right side out and press.
5. Mark the following positions along the lengthwise edges:
- Left side: 1", 3", 6", and 12" (2.5 cm, 7.5 cm, 15 cm, and 30.5 cm).
- Right side: 2", 4", 8", and 16" (5 cm, 10 cm, 20.5 cm, and 40.5 cm).
6. Machine-bar-tack at each marking, stitching close to the lengthwise edges (Diagram C).
7. Form the bow by pulling the ribbons taut. Shape and fluff the Tack-a-Bloom (Diagram D). Tie the bow on package.

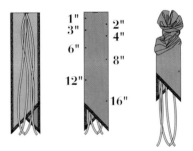

**Diagram B    Diagram C    Diagram D**

### Tip from Gail

Slip a tassel on a gift for instant elegance. Stock up on purchased tassels to match your wraps, or make your own from serged thread chains (see page 133).

# Fabric "Ribbon"

No ribbon? Gather remnants of soft, light-reflective fabric such as lining, lamé, satin, taffeta, tulle, or netting. Then get ready for fast ribbon-making.

- **For tubes:** Cut 2"- to 10"-wide (5 cm- to 25.5 cm-wide) strips. Piece together strips to achieve the desired length. See page 135 for how to seam and turn tubes. Finish the ends by softly knotting them or tucking them inside the tube *(Diagram A).* Optional: Hand-gather the ends and sew metal bells to cover the stitches.

balanced stitch, piece together the short ends to achieve the desired length *(Diagram B).* Serge-finish all edges. (For serging tips, see page 132.)

## Easy Box Embellishments

- Using fabric glue or a glue gun, glue shank buttons to the box top. Optional: Space buttons to allow for a ribbon tie.
- Tie with a Fabric "Ribbon" *(photo below).*

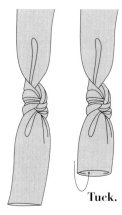

**Tuck.**

**Diagram A**

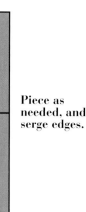

**Piece as needed, and serge edges.**

**Diagram B**

- **For sashes:** Cut 2"- to 6"-wide (5 cm- to 15 cm-wide) strips. Remember that lengthwise-grain strips serge-finish more neatly than crosswise-grain strips. Using a narrow rolled or

# Bonus Project: "I Love to Sew" Accents

Keep tomato pincushions and strawberry emery cushions on hand to use as clever package accents. Embellish the cushions with ribbons or buttons, if desired. Use a fabric marking pen to write your gift message directly on the cushion surface, or pin on a paper or fabric gift tag. What better way to embellish a fabric-wrapped gift, while saying "I love to sew"?

*Now your tags can match your fabric wrap perfectly. All you need are fabric scraps, remnants of wrapping paper, and small pieces of paper-backed fusible web.*

## Fabric Gift Tags

- Fuse paper-backed fusible web to the wrong side of your fabric and remove the paper.
- With little or no steam, fuse the fabric to the wrong side of gift wrap *(Diagram A)*.
- Using a rotary cutter with a straight, wave, or pinking blade, trim the tag into any card shape. Fold or use flat.
- Use a paper punch to make a hole *(Diagram B)*.
- Optional: Thread the hole with ribbon, and tie the tag onto a package *(Diagram C)*. Or pin the tag on a Dimensional Ornament (page 85), a pincushion, or a strawberry emery cushion accent (see "I Love to Sew" accents bonus project).

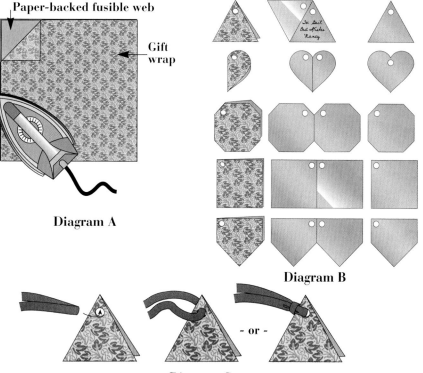

Paper-backed fusible web

Gift wrap

**Diagram A**

**Diagram B**

- or -

**Diagram C**

Workshop

# Appliqué

*Tot's Getup (page 22) uses appliquéd facial features.*

## Gather Supplies
- Paper-backed fusible web
- Fabric scraps for appliqués: cotton, velour, fleece, Ultrasuede®
- Tear-away stabilizer
- Open toe presser foot
- Embroidery thread
- Lingerie/Bobbin Thread
- Machine embroidery needle, size 75
- Optional: Water-soluble stabilizer for Ultrasuede or terry cloth
- Optional: Adhesive web for Ultrasuede
- Optional: Microtex machine needle for Ultrasuede

## Stitch Appliqués
1. Apply paper-backed fusible web to the fabric scraps.
- Trace the designs on the paper side of paper-backed fusible web.
- Roughly cut out the shapes, leaving a ½" (13 cm) margin around each shape.
- Following the manufacturer's directions, fuse the shapes to the wrong side of the appliqué fabric.

2. Cut out the shapes and peel away the paper backing.
3. Place the appliqués, fusible side down, on the project. Cover appliqués with a damp cloth and fuse.
4. Place tear-away stabilizer under the appliqué.
5. Adjust the sewing machine for satin stitching.
- Replace the foot with an open toe embroidery/appliqué foot. The underside of this foot is grooved to allow stitches to pass easily under the presser foot. The wide opening makes it easier to see the stitching *(Diagram A)*.

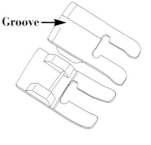

**Diagram A**

- Thread the top of the machine with embroidery thread; use a lightweight thread in the bobbin.
- Insert a machine embroidery needle.
- Slightly loosen the top tension (by two numbers) so that the bobbin thread remains on the underside of the fabric.
- Select a short stitch length (.5) and a medium stitch width.
6. Satin-stitch the appliqué edges.
- Stitch so that one edge of the zigzag catches the appliqué and the other edge stitches just past the raw edge of the appliqué.
- To make it easier to pivot the fabric, adjust the machine so that the needle stops in the down position, if possible.
- To stitch outside corners, sew to the corner, stopping at the

corner, with the needle in the outside position. Raise the presser foot and pivot the fabric. Lower the presser foot and continue stitching *(Diagram B)*.

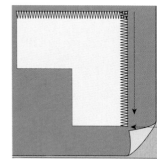

Stop with needle in outside position.

**Diagram B**

- To stitch inside corners, stitch the width of the zigzag stitch beyond the corner. Stop with the needle in the inside position. Raise the presser foot and pivot the fabric; lower the foot and continue stitching *(Diagram C)*.

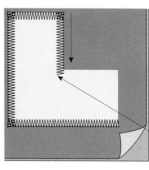

Stitch beyond corner.

**Diagram C**

- To stitch curves, stop with the needle on the outside when stitching outside curves, and on the inside when stitching inside curves *(Diagram D)*.

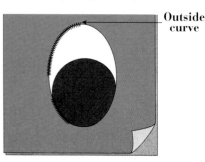

Outside curve

**Diagram D**

7. Carefully tear away stabilizer.

## Appliqué Tips for Terry Cloth or Turkish Towels

To stitch appliqués on terry cloth or Turkish towels (such as those shown on pages 22–26), follow general appliqué instructions with these guidelines:

- Place a layer of water-soluble stabilizer, such as Avalon by Madeira, on top of the appliqués. This clear stabilizer prevents the nap from getting caught in the toes of the presser foot. You can draw facial features, such as eyelashes, on the stabilizer to provide a guide for satin stitching.
- If small pieces of stabilizer remain after you tear it away, remove them by dipping the area in water or pressing with a damp press cloth.

## Appliqué Tips for Ultrasuede

Ultrasuede is a nonraveling, washable synthetic suede fabric. To use it for appliqués, follow general appliqué directions with the following guidelines:

- Cut appliqués from Ultrasuede pieces. They're less expensive than yardage and are usually sold in 6" x 9" (15 cm x 23 cm) and 9" x 12" (23 cm x 30.5 cm) sizes.
- Use a pressure-sensitive adhesive web, such as AppliqEase™. This web eliminates the last pressing step, preventing damage to Ultrasuede's nap.

### Note from Nancy

AppliqEase is a press-on backing that's especially useful for appliqués made from surface-sensitive fabrics, such as Ultrasuede. Simply fuse AppliqEase to appliqué fabric, and remove the paper backing to reveal a sticky surface.

- Use a Microtex machine needle to prevent skipped stitches.
- Edgestitch Ultrasuede appliqués using a short stitch length, such as 12 stitches to the inch (2.5) *(Diagram)*. A shorter stitch makes it easier to sew smooth curves.

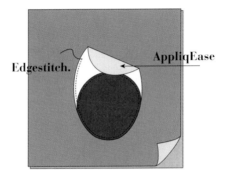

Edgestitch.  AppliqEase

**Diagram**

### Note from Nancy

We used Ultrasuede appliqués on the Tot's Getup (page 22). The feet and tail don't require satin stitching because Ultrasuede doesn't ravel. We straight-stitched around the edges of the features when we used two layers of Ultrasuede.

# Fusible Interfacing

## Gather Supplies

- Fusible interfacing slightly lighter than your fabric. For example, if you're using medium-weight fabric, choose lightweight fusible interfacing. Fusing resins add weight you probably won't notice until after fusing.
- Press cloth

## Fuse Interfacing to Fabric

1. Center interfacing on the fabric, placing the interfacing's resin side next to the wrong side of the fabric.
2. Steam-baste the interfacing in place before permanently fusing. To do this, use the tip of your iron to secure it to the fabric in a few key areas.
3. Fuse the interfacing following the manufacturer's instructions. (General guidelines follow.) Press with an up-and-down motion.

- Set the iron at wool temperature.
- Protect the fabric and interfacing with a press cloth. By using a transparent press cloth, you can see the fabric while fusing.
- Use steam or dampen the press cloth.
- Fuse for 10 to 15 seconds.
- Apply sufficient pressure. This is the most important step, but it is often overlooked. If the fabric has a bubbly appearance after fusing, you probably didn't press hard enough. Try fusing again, adding more pressure.

# Bias Binding

*Contrasting bias binding dresses up the edges of this Photo Wallet (page 103).*

## Gather Supplies
- Rotary cutter, ruler, and mat
- Fabric
- Thread to match
- Optional: Bias Tape Maker

## Prepare Binding
1. Cut 2"-wide (5 cm-wide) bias strips, using a rotary cutter, ruler, and mat *(Diagram A)*.

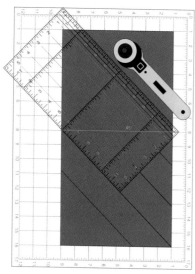

**Diagram A**

2. Join the strips to make a binding.
- Place one strip on a flat surface, right side up.
- Lay a second strip perpendicular to the first, right sides together. Offset strips about ¼" (6 mm).

Stitch the strips together, making a diagonal seam *(Diagram B)*.

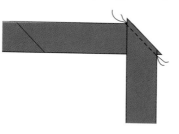

**Diagram B**

3. Press the seam open *(Diagram C)*.

**Diagram C**

4. Trim away the V-shaped corners at the intersections.
5. Repeat until you make enough yardage to bind all project edges.

## Create Bias Tape
1. Turn under the cut edges to form bias tape, following either Step 2 or Step 3 below.
2. Use a Bias Tape Maker.
- Insert the bias strip, wrong side up, through the wide end of a 1" (25 mm) Bias Tape Maker.
- Use a pin to advance the fabric through the tape maker's wide end. The fabric edges will fold to the middle as they come out the narrow end *(photo below)*. Press.

**Bias Tape Maker**

3. Use an iron.
- With wrong sides together, fold the strip in half lengthwise and lightly press to mark a center line
- Fold the cut edges to the center mark. Press *(Diagram D)*.

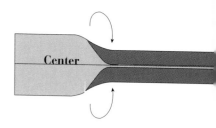

**Diagram D**

- To make double-fold tape, align the folded edges and press again.

## Attach Binding
1. Pin the bias tape to the project.
- Unfold one lengthwise edge of the bias tape. With edges even, place the right side of the tape next to the wrong side of the project.
- In curved areas, gently mold the tape to conform to the edge so that both the tape and the project remain flat.
- Turn under the short edge of the bias tape ¼" (6 mm) and pin *(Diagram E)*.

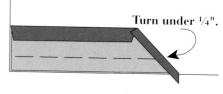

Turn under ¼".

**Diagram E**

2. Stitch the bias tape to the project, sewing just inside the first press mark *(Diagram F)*.

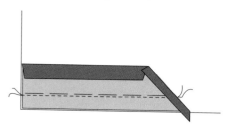

**Diagram F**

3. Where the tape ends meet, overlap the free end ¼" (6 mm) onto the stitched-down section. Cut off any excess tape.

• From the right side, machine-stitch or handstitch the intersection of the tape ends together. Because the intersection is on the bias, it will be inconspicuous (*Diagram G*).

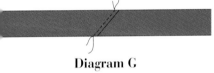

**Diagram G**

• Wrap the tape to the right side of the project, aligning the tape's folded edge with the stitching line. Pin.

• Working from the right side, handstitch or machine-edgestitch the tape in place (*Diagram H*).

**Diagram H**

# Gathering

## Gather Supplies
• Fabric
• Thread to match
• Optional: cording or dental floss

## Create Gathering

1. Place the fabric underneath the presser foot. Turn the wheel by hand to take one complete stitch in the fabric. Bring the bobbin thread to the top side by lightly pulling on it. The bobbin thread will appear as a loop coming through the fabric (*Diagram AA*).

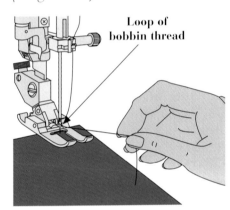

**Diagram AA**

2. Pull the bobbin and the top threads to measure as long as the area to be gathered. Gently twist the threads together (*Diagram BB*).

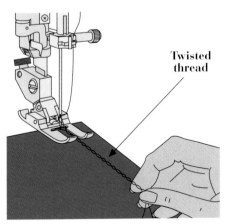

**Diagram BB**

3. Adjust your machine for a wide zigzag and a short stitch length. Stitch over the twisted threads inside the seam allowance, making a casing for the gathered threads. Make sure you don't stitch through the twisted threads (*Diagram CC*).

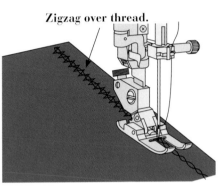

**Diagram CC**

4. Pull the twisted threads to gather. Because the threads are anchored in the first stitch, the gathering threads will not pull out of the fabric (*Diagram DD*).

**Diagram DD**

# Serging Basics

*Serged edges like those for this unlined Furoshiki wrap (page 116) are both attractive and functional.*

## Basic Serger Stitches

### Gather Supplies
- All-purpose serger thread
- Narrow rolled-edge foot, and/or throat plate
- Optional: Woolly Nylon thread

### 3-Thread Overlock Stitch
In this stitch, the threads interlock with the needle thread on the left. The upper and lower looper threads interlock at the fabric's edge *(Diagram A)*. When the looper tensions are balanced, the stitch looks the same on both sides. The 3-thread overlock stitch, generally used for seaming or edge finishing, is stretchy, which makes it ideal for seaming knits. It's also a useful stitch for decorative serging. Try heavier threads, ribbons, or yarns in the loopers.

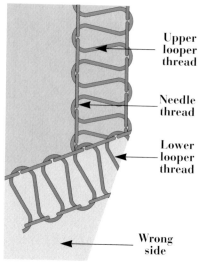

Diagram A

Labels: Upper looper thread; Needle thread; Lower looper thread; Wrong side

### 3/4-Thread Overlock Stitch
A 3/4 thread overlock stitch adds a second needle line to the right of the primary seam line. The second line of thread runs through both loopers, creating a stitch that is more stable and durable than the 3-thread stitch *(Diagram B)*.

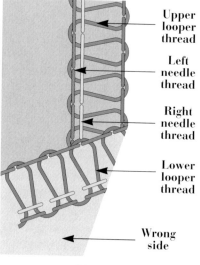

Diagram B

Labels: Upper looper thread; Left needle thread; Right needle thread; Lower looper thread; Wrong side

### Narrow Rolled-Edge Stitch
To create this stitch, a 3-thread overlock stitch is converted to a narrow rolled-edge stitch. Tension adjustments are crucial! Listed below are guidelines for converting a 3-thread stitch into a narrow rolled-edge stitch *(Diagram C)*. Check your owner's manual for the exact settings for your serger, or if you prefer a 2-thread rolled edge.

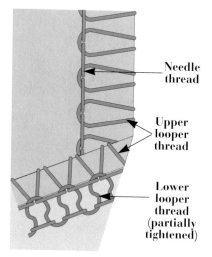

Diagram C

Labels: Needle thread; Upper looper thread; Lower looper thread (partially tightened)

1. Replace the standard serger foot with the narrow rolled-edge foot, which has a narrower stitch finger *(Diagram D)*. On some sergers, the stitch finger is on a separate throat plate instead of on the presser foot; if your serger has this feature, change the throat plate. Other sergers require changing both the foot and the throat plate. On some sergers, you must drop part of the stitch finger, rather than change either the foot or the plate.

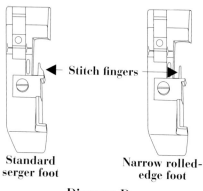

Stitch fingers

Standard serger foot

Narrow rolled-edge foot

Diagram D

2. Narrow the stitch width (usually as much as possible) and shorten the stitch length. Begin with a setting of 2 mm for the stitch length, adjusting as necessary to achieve the desired coverage and tension.
3. If you are using a 3/4-thread serger, remove the left needle.
4. Adjust the tensions.
  Tighten the lower-looper tension considerably.
• Loosen the upper-looper tension. Test the stitch and adjust the tensions as necessary to achieve the desired look. With the upper-looper tension loosened and the lower-looper tension tightened, the upper-looper thread should roll over the edge. You may need to widen the "bite," or stitch width, to roll more fabric within the stitch and prevent raveling.
5. If serging over fishing line or lightweight wire (see page 116), use a cording or beading foot to help guide the filler under the looper.

## Narrow Unrolled Edge

To serge a narrow unrolled edge, use the narrow rolled-edge foot, but leave the tension balanced. A narrow unrolled edge is the perfect serger stitch to use when a fabric is particularly resistant to rolling.

## Lettuce Edges

Create serged "lettuce curls" on the edges of stretchy fabrics, such as the crosswise grain of interlock, ribbing, fleece, or Lycra-blend knits (see project on left in large photo, page 119). Adjust your serger for a narrow rolled-edge stitch and a short stitch length. Stretch fabric in front of and behind the presser foot while serging, and be careful not to bend the needle. If your machine has differential feed, set it on the lowest or "minus" setting.

*Custom-serge your own tassels for perfect color coordination.*

## Serged-Chain Tassels

1. After finishing a project with narrow rolled edges, continue to serge, pulling the threads taut behind the foot, until you create a chain 6 to 8 yards (5.50 m to 7.35 m) long. Using decorative threads in either or both loopers produces a more decorative tassel.
2. Loosely wind the chain over a firm piece of cardboard (package inserts from sewing trim work well). The more chain you wrap, the fuller the tassel.
3. Tie an 8" (20.5 cm) double strand of chain around one end of the cardboard, and dab seam sealant on the chains on the opposite end *(Diagram AA)*. Let dry. Cut through the sealed chains along the edge of the cardboard. Make sure that seam sealant remains on both cut portions.

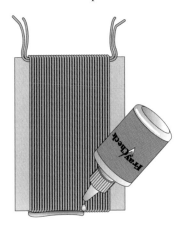

**Diagram AA**

4. Measure 1" (2.5 cm) below tied end and wrap with a thread chain. Knot and bury the chain underneath the wraps *(Diagram BB)*.

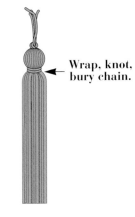

→ **Wrap, knot, bury chain.**

**Diagram BB**

# Machine-Sewn Piping

*Piping emphasizes the seams of the One-Piece Chevron Pillow (page 74).*

## Gather Supplies
- Piping or cording presser foot
- Fabric
- ⅛"-diameter (3.2 mm-diameter) cording
- Thread to match

### Note from Nancy

You can save time by buying 1" (25.4 mm) piping. Simply sew the tape portion into the seam line as described in Step 2.

## Create Machine-Sewn Piping
1. Make piping.
- Cut bias strips 2" to 2½" (5 cm to 6.3 cm) wide by the needed length. Cut the cording the same length. (See page 130.)

---

- Attach the cording foot to your sewing machine. The foot's groove saves a step, making insertion a one-step rather than a two-step process *(Diagram A)*. If you don't have a cording foot, see *Tip from Gail* after Step 2.

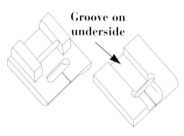

**Diagram A**

- With wrong sides together, fold the bias strip lengthwise, sandwiching the cording in the fold.
- Position the cording to fit in the groove of the foot *(Diagram B)*.

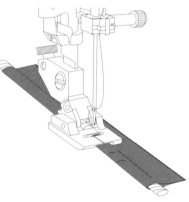

**Diagram B**

- Adjust the sewing machine needle to stitch close to the edge of the cording. Stitch.
- Trim ⅝" (1.5 cm) from stitching line to make the piping seam allowance match the project seam allowance *(Diagram C)*.

**Diagram C**

---

2. Stitch the piping into the seam.
- With right sides together and raw edges even, sandwich the piping seam allowance between the two project seam allowances
- Place the piping in the groove of the cording foot. Stitch through all layers *(Diagram D)*.

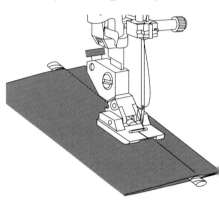

**Diagram D**

### Tip from Gail

You can use a zipper foot to apply piping or cording. Replace your sewing machine's regular presser foot with the zipper foot, which allows you to sew very close to the piping. Sew the piping to one side of the seam first, then sew the seam using the first row of stitching as a guide.

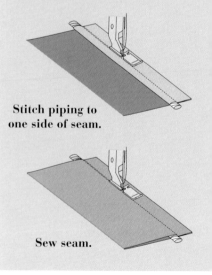

**Stitch piping to one side of seam.**

**Sew seam.**

# Other Basics

## Fabric Tubes

### Gather Supplies
- Fasturn tube turner
- Fabric
- Thread to match

### Create Fabric Tubes
1. Cut strips of fabric twice the width of the finished tube plus ½" (1.3 cm) for seam allowances.
2. With right sides together, stitch the lengthwise edges with a ¼" (6 mm) seam.
3. Turn the tubes right side out.
- Thread the tube over the Fasturn cylinder, wrapping the end of the tube over the cylinder.
- Push Fasturn's pigtail wire into the cylinder from the handle end.
- Turn the wire clockwise, pushing the pigtail through the fabric.
- Gently pull the wire back through the cylinder, turning the tube right side out.
- Release the wire from the tube by turning the wire counter-clockwise *(Diagram AA)*.

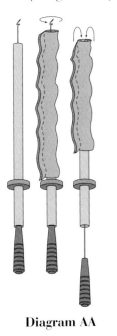

**Diagram AA**

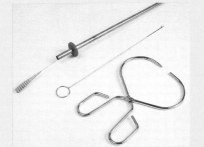

## Stitching-in-the-Ditch

To stitch-in-the-ditch, stitch in the groove (called the well or the ditch) of a seam on the right side of the garment. Sew through all thicknesses *(Diagram BB)*.

**Diagram BB**

## Clean-Finished Edges

There are several ways to finish raw edges of fabric (see pages 33–35), but clean finishing is one of the simplest methods.
1. Zigzag or serge the fabric edge.
2. Press the stitched edge under ¼" (6 mm) to the wrong side.
3. Topstitch in place *(Diagram CC)*.

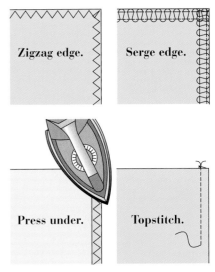

Zigzag edge.

Serge edge.

Press under.

Topstitch.

**Diagram CC**

## Double Hem

A double hem keeps edges from showing through sheer fabrics, and it adds weight to hems.

To create a double hem, make the hem allowance twice the desired finished depth. Fold up the hem along the hemline. Then fold the hem allowance under so that the raw edges are next to the hemline.
- To stitch a hem by machine, topstitch or use a blindhem stitch. Double-needle topstitching makes a nice finish for knits.
- To stitch a hem by hand, use a blindhem stitch, a slipstitch, or a catchstitch.
- To fuse a double hem, cut strips of fusible web equal to the hem depth. Fuse the right side of the hem allowance to the wrong side of the garment.

# Patterns

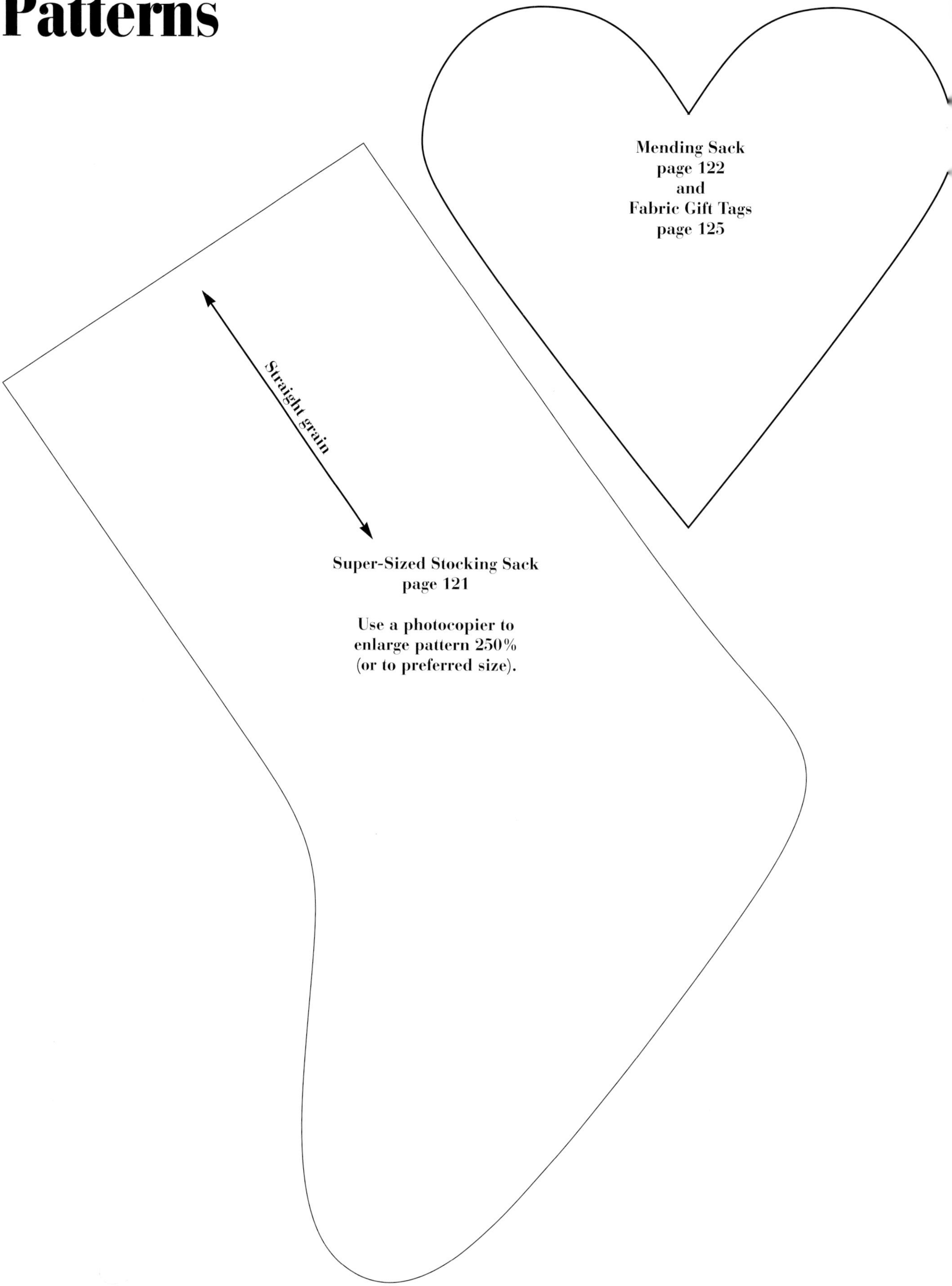

**Mending Sack
page 122
and
Fabric Gift Tags
page 125**

Straight grain

**Super-Sized Stocking Sack
page 121**

**Use a photocopier to
enlarge pattern 250%
(or to preferred size).**

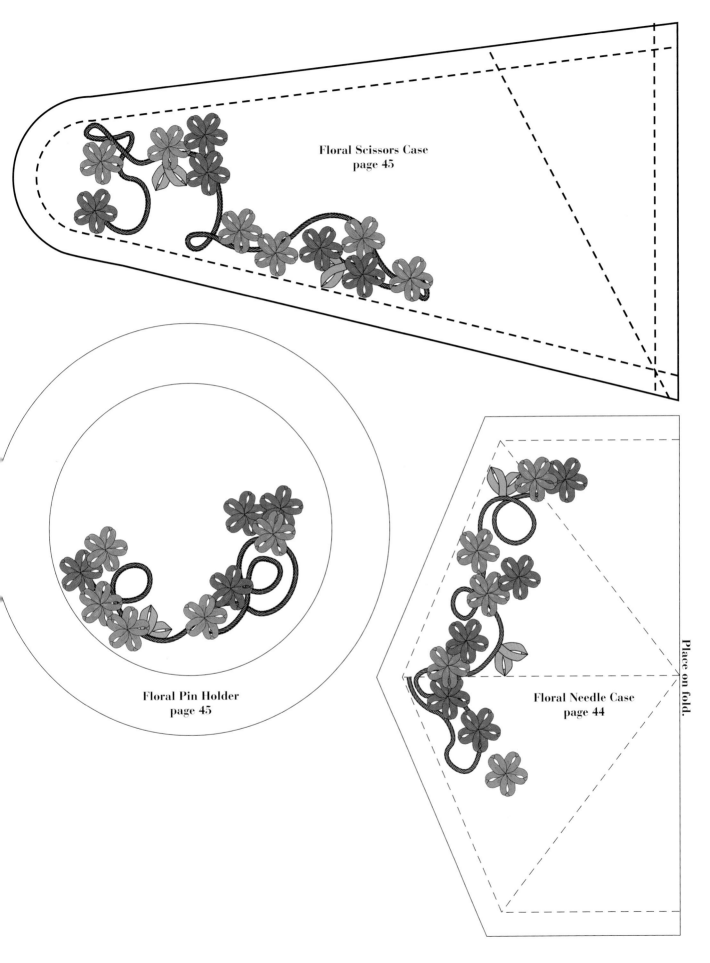

Floral Scissors Case
page 45

Floral Pin Holder
page 45

Floral Needle Case
page 44

Place on fold.

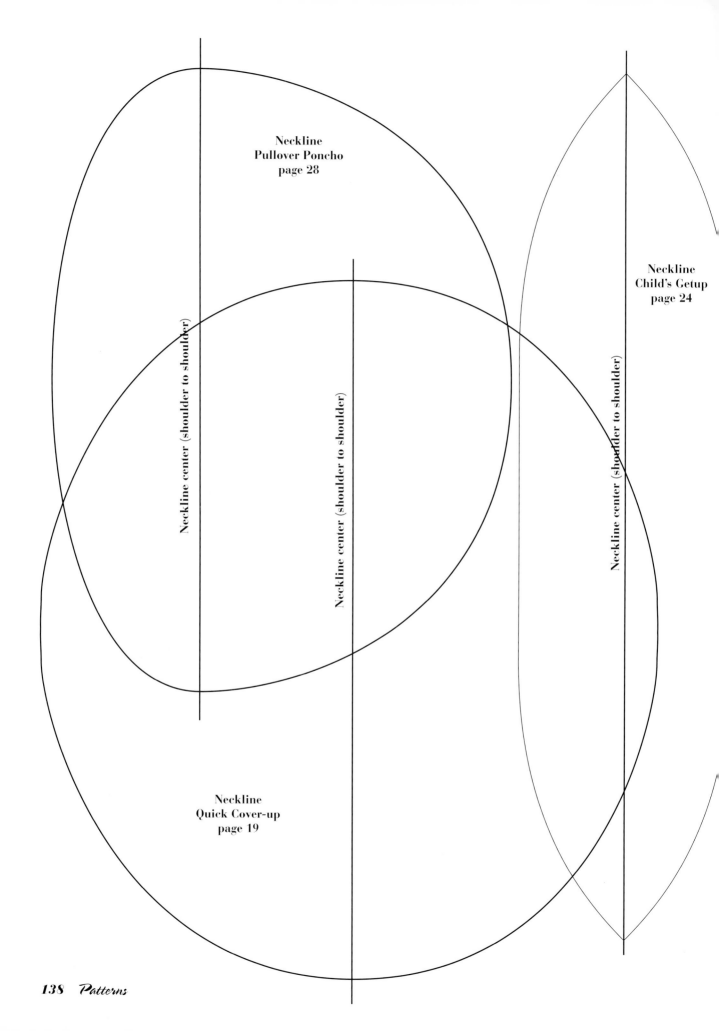

Neckline
Pullover Poncho
page 28

Neckline
Child's Getup
page 24

Neckline center (shoulder to shoulder)

Neckline center (shoulder to shoulder)

Neckline center (shoulder to shoulder)

Neckline
Quick Cover-up
page 19

Cow
Tot's Getup
page 22
and
Child's Getup
page 24

Use a photocopier to
enlarge pattern 185%
(or to preferred size).

Tail

Hoof

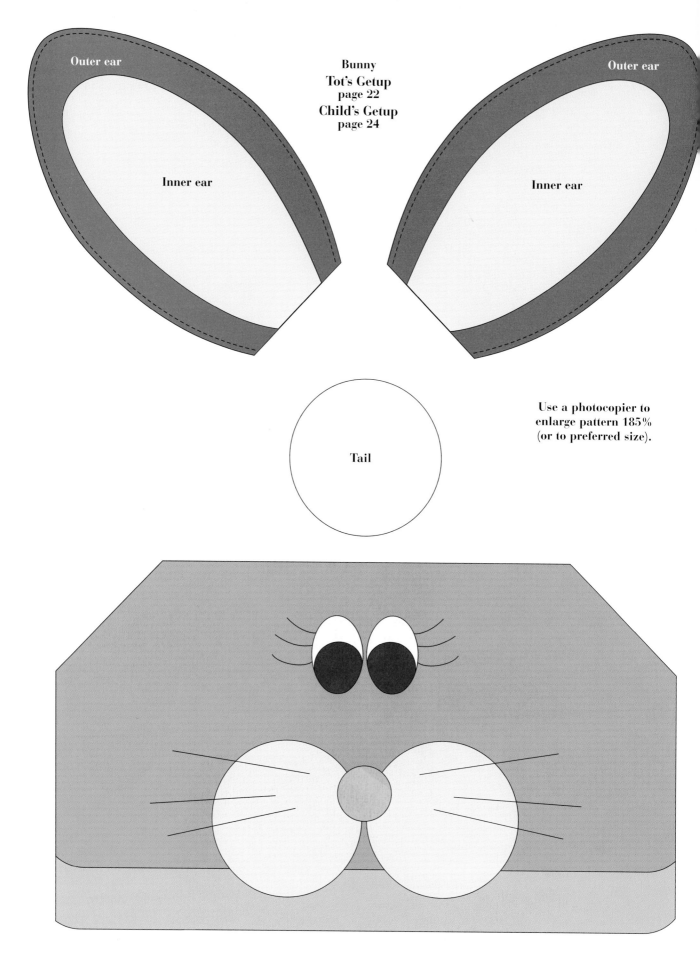

Outer ear

Inner ear

Bunny
**Tot's Getup**
page 22
**Child's Getup**
page 24

Outer ear

Inner ear

Tail

Use a photocopier to
enlarge pattern 185%
(or to preferred size).

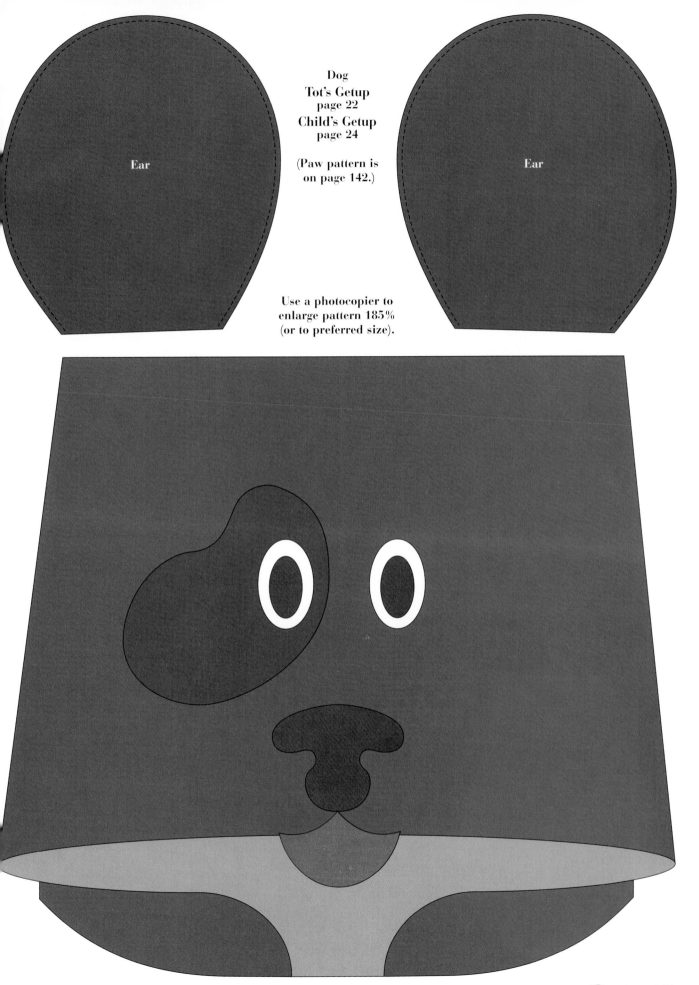

**Dog**
**Tot's Getup**
page 22
**Child's Getup**
page 24

(Paw pattern is
on page 142.)

Ear

Ear

Use a photocopier to
enlarge pattern 185%
(or to preferred size).

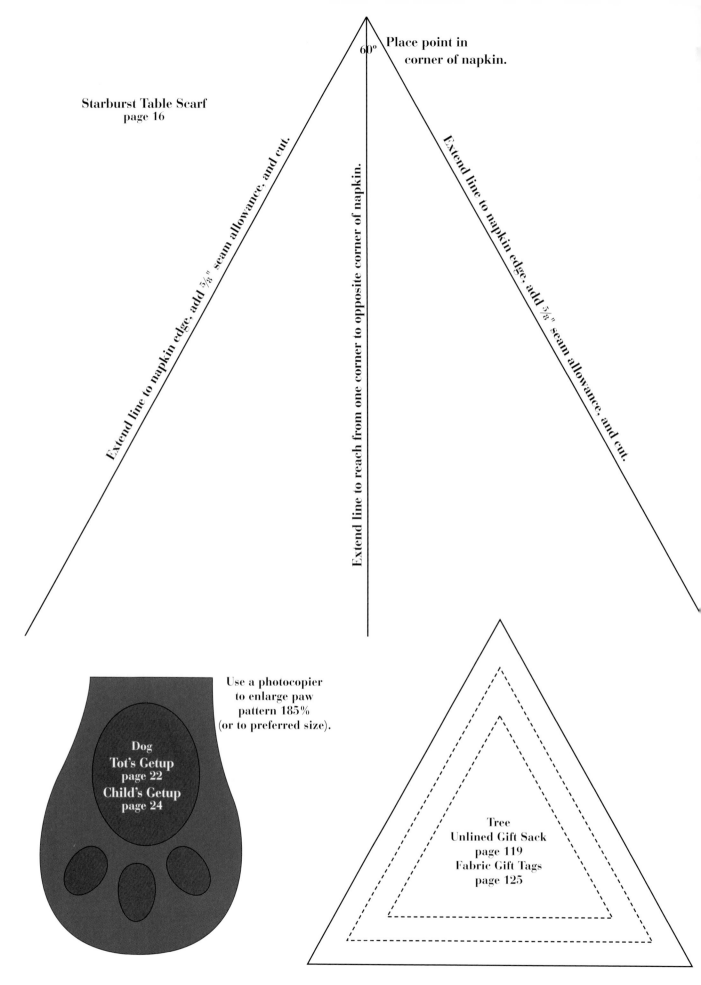

**Starburst Table Scarf**
page 16

60°  Place point in
corner of napkin.

Extend line to napkin edge, add ⅝" seam allowance, and cut.

Extend line to reach from one corner to opposite corner of napkin.

Extend line to napkin edge, add ⅝" seam allowance, and cut.

Use a photocopier
to enlarge paw
pattern 185%
(or to preferred size).

**Dog**
**Tot's Getup**
page 22
**Child's Getup**
page 24

**Tree**
**Unlined Gift Sack**
page 119
**Fabric Gift Tags**
page 125

# Index

*Denotes Bonus Project*

# Nancy Zieman

Businesswoman, home economist, and national sewing authority, Nancy Zieman is producer and hostess of the popular show "Sewing With Nancy," which appears exclusively on public television stations. The show, broadcast since September 1982, is the longest-airing sewing program on television.

Nancy also produces and hosts Sewing With Nancy videos. Currently, there are 28 one-hour videos available to retailers, educators, libraries, and sewing groups. In addition, she is founder and president of Nancy's Notions, Ltd., a mail-order sewing notions company, which publishes Nancy's Notions Sewing Catalog. This large catalog contains more than 4,000 products, including sewing books, notions, videos, and fabrics.

Nancy has written several books, including: *Essential Sewing Guide, Sew Easy Embellishments, Fitting Finesse, 501 Sewing Hints,* and *Sewing Express.* In each book, she emphasizes efficient sewing techniques that produce professional results.

The Wisconsin Women Entrepreneurs Association named Nancy 1988 Entrepreneurial Woman of the Year. In 1991, she also received the National 4-H Alumni Award. She is a member of the American Association of Family and Consumer Sciences and the American Home Sewing & Crafts Association.

Nancy lives in Beaver Dam, Wisconsin, with her husband and business partner, Rich, and their two sons, Ted and Tom.

# Gail Brown

With 11 books and hundreds of articles to her credit, Gail Brown ranks as one of the most widely read sewing journalists. She is well known for her unique projects and techniques that emphasize "easy but elegant."

Her work has appeared in *Woman's Day Specials, Sew News, The Singer Sewing Library, Sewing Update Newsletter,* and *Serger Update Newsletter.* She also appears often on the "Sewing With Nancy" public television show, in Nancy's Notions Ltd. videos, and on the Home & Garden Television (HGTV) show, "Sew Perfect." Gail has also appeared on segments for "Our Home" through Viacom/ Lifetime Television.

Gail's book, *The Ultimate Serger Answer Guide,* which covers serger troubleshooting, won the prestigious Product Excellence Award at the 1997 Hobby Industries of America convention. Her columns appear on the Nancy's Notions World Wide Web page (www.nancysnotions.com).

Although this home economics graduate started her career in New York City's garment district, she now works out of her home office in the small coastal town of Hoquiam, Washington. She lives with her husband, John Quigg, their children, Bett and Jack, and a huge stash of sewing supplies.